BERNARD VENABLES

The Illustrated Memoirs of a Fisherman

Merlin Unwin Books

Bernard Venables

THE ILLUSTRATED MEMOIRS OF A FISHERMAN

Copyright details

Contents

Acknowledgements

I am indebted to many people who have helped in putting together this book. In particular to my friends Mark and Jackie Williams who have been so kind in assembling and accomodating many of the paintings that appear within these pages, and then allowing their house to be used as a photographic studio. Jackie deserves a special medal for typing out my original manuscript. Many others have generously allowed paintings of mine to be photographed for inclusion in this book. I would like to specially thank James Arnold-Baker, Mark and Jackie Williams, Bill Beale Collins, Stella Zweck, and Richard Nicoll - all of whom have kindly allowed piantings in their possession to be reproduced here. Forbes Stephenson, the photographer, whose task it was to record on film all these paintings did so most professionally on that hot day in June at East Grafton.

My old employers, *The Mirror*, have kindly allowed some of the Crabtree illustrations to be reproduced. Neil Pope, editor of *Improve Your Coarse Fishing* (in my view the best new fishing magazine on the market) has been wonderfully supportive both to me and to this book. Peter Rogers, who lent a picture for reproducton, has also been particularly generous in his help and support for this project. If there are others that I have missed out then the fault is mine, and I thank them too.

Recently, I have had much fun visiting some old fishing haunts with Chris Yates and Bob James (we are photographed together on the back jacket) and being filmed doing so by that wonderful cameraman Hugh Miles. It will be amusing to see our escapades in the forthcoming BBC film *A Passion for Angling*.

Last, but by no means least, I wish to thank my wife Eileen whose constant support and encouragement has been fundamental to this book and to my continuing happiness as a fisher-artist.

Bernard Venables, Upavon, Wiltshire
January 1993

Colour illustrations

Black and white illustrations

Foreword

This book is a rather random record of a long life; it is a record of much living having been done, and much still to do. I suppose it has been in one respect a fortunate one, because at no time in history has there been so much almost unimaginable change; nowhere has that change been greater than in those things which have been the substance of my life. In art, in fishing, in man's relationship with nature, there has been change revolutionary beyond any other period in the world's history.

When I was born, this century was seven years old. River flow was undiminished, and it had not yet occurred to anyone to draw away a river's life even before it emerged from its hidden sources deep under the chalk or limestone. Much coarse fishing water was still freely to be had, and where charge was made it was modest enough for anyone. Ditches, little streams, all sorts of minor waterways hardly outside big towns, still swarmed with minnows, sticklebacks and often gudgeon too, so that small boys in whom there was the urge could have a first taste of catching living, pulsing little fish. There were still ponds, unconsidered lakes, canals to which they could turn next, to catch those intoxicating little perch and roach, so taking youngsters on their way to becoming grown-up anglers.

How simple, how very innocent the fishing of that time - so immensely long ago in effect, but not really many years past. It would probably be hard to convince young anglers of today that they could be wholly fulfilled and happy in their fishing without all the technological wonders of tackle that nowadays are assumed to be essential.

However, that instinct which makes anglers of men is very strong - it is fundamental. I think, and hope, it may be stronger than the shallow and probably fugitive wonder of modern tackle technology, and the gamesmanship that has come into angling in the past thirty or forty years. If we can save our waters from all that threatens them, I think the older, simpler joy of angling can regain its hold.

It might even be that this small survey of one very long angling life may help to give a longer and more helpful view.

One of the oldest stories in fishing: the proverbial tale of the boy who takes the great specimen fish that eludes his elders. Like most quaint fishing tales told by non-fishermen, it is only rarely true. But just occasionally, it does happen. I can well remember just such a boy - a great poacher that lad was!

A Prospect of Angling

I cannot be said ever to have become an angler - just as I cannot be said ever to have become an artist. Awareness of both came with my first consciousness. I remember nothing earlier than the urge to do both. Chance for the doing, for angling anyway, had to wait; there was no water within my constricted reach for the possibility of fishing. But the urge, the consciousness of living water, was insistent. My inward eye was constant with visions of fish gliding within the water's mystery. My first opportunity to broach the water's hypnotic mystery did not come until the advanced age of six. Then, of course, it was no more than the stick and string and penny hook which was the norm for beginners of my time; but it was a beginning. In deed, if not in reward, I was now a proven angler.

That was a long time ago; 80 years ago. In that time a very great deal has happened both to angling and to art. Not all change in fishing has been for the worse. The same cannot be said of art.

Having so long a perspective, so long a time of seeing and of doing, surely gives me a more than usual qualification for assessment. The world of fishing of those beginning times is so much more distant than just the total of the years. By contrast with today it was archaic; for many of today's unquestioned essentials for fishing had not then been thought of. Were we then, in the eyes of today, deprived? We were not. Passionately it must be said that we were not. We had not the faintest sense that we lacked the blessings that so astonishingly fill the tackle shops of the present and make such material for hyper-technical talk.

What had we then? Let it be seen what were the constituents of our fishing. The water? Of that there was abundance. Some waters, affected by pollution then, have since been restored to a fishable state. But that is minimal compared with what has since been lost.

At the age of six, I was living on Romney Marsh in Kent. I could walk across the narrow 'main' road to the dyke which ran brimming there, to attempt to catch its fish. That road now is wide and roars with traffic. The dyke has gone; the marsh has been drained and made into football pitches. Many of the ponds in many places, which in those far-off days gave me my first success with little fish, have gone. Abstraction has drained many rivers and desperately threatened many others.

Our fishing was quiet; it lay in sweet meadows; its peace was untouched. Much coarse fishing was to be had just for the free taking. Even in the time of the second Great War there were tangled brooks, not far from London, where anyone could catch the little wild trout. About that long-gone fishing there was ease, an absence of competitiveness, no taint of striving. A day was considered perfect in which, all day, we had been watching a red-topped float that occasionally dipped to a quite moderately-sized fish. We, as must all anglers, were always in hope of that rare big fish; but equally we knew that happiness could be found without such triumph. For me, fishing's real delight lay in its Eden-like atmosphere, in the blissful hypnosis of the water's mystery.

And tackle? Ours then, I suppose, would seem ludicrous now. Who now could comprehend the pleasure of possession of a wooden reel? Or rods of mottled cane or brittle lancewood? For us, who then were young probationers, lines were normally brown thread. It was later sophistication that brought those of silk which were fine by earlier standards. Those silk lines - how treasured they were. After every use they had to be dried on line driers. Or, more often, wound on a chair-back to dry. And fly lines; even greater care they demanded. They were of silk, dressed with oil to give them their final snake-like, luscious texture. They were lovely, inviting to the touch. But neglect them and the demon tackiness would pounce. There was no cure: alleged cures there were, involving use of talc, French chalk, this and that, but all in vain.

Then, our casts. In those days nobody had started calling them leaders. They were of silkworm gut, and that came to us rebelliously brittle; a cast damper was standard equipment. The coiled cast was put between the two wet felt discs about half-an-hour before fishing, thus making the gut tractable and fit for knotting. Or there was gut substitute, man-made, but it too needed soaking. It was more particularly used as a line for fixed-spool reels - but that was a very latter-day device, very modern; we were using it in the 1930s.

So, as it may be seen now, we were very disadvantaged in tackle. But we did not know we were. We were entirely happy with our tackle. We had as much gloating pleasure in it as in any wonder

of today. Our fishing pleasure then was simple, unsophisticated, but it was intense. It had no cults. In our timeless days we smelt the river scent, we heard the breeze fingering through the trees, we heard the birds; sometimes in the drifting hours the float would dip. On occasions we caught big fish - among our placid days we had our red-letter days.

The end of the second Great War brought the first changes. They were dramatic and very welcome. Those heaven-sent new materials; how difficult now to recall the old world in which there was no nylon and no plastic. No more had we to strip all the line from our reels for drying after fishing, no more soaking of gut, no more greasing of fly lines. The new lines, quite soon after the war, were self-floating (and we were suspicious of them at first). All those wonderful innovations - and this is perhaps inevitable, since that whole world too is dead and distant - have an old, naive look.

That apparent post-war burst of change was no more than a prelude to what was to come. But it was a very happy time - the old simplicities were not lost. Fishing waters had not deteriorated seriously; it was very pleasurable to have the help of the new tackle, and we were still in the age of split cane. Indeed, though brief, this was the golden age of split cane. Among the new discoveries was miracle glue. With that and improved techniques, built cane rods attained final perfection.

Now, it seemed, we had everything. Fishing had reached its zenith. Looking back I am inclined to think it had - in terms of the marriage of angling skills and the most beautifully-efficient artifacts. As yet there was no hint of marring that marriage by technology's cold touch. The progress was clearly to be seen from the *Treatyse of Fysshynge Wyth An Angle* of 1496, up through the centuries, generation by generation adding to our arts and mysteries. It was a happy state.

But technology was already taking its first tentative steps. Gaining momentum, it created new attitudes of mind. Technology, soon, was the new god: it gathered worshippers. The movement of emphasis from the dominance of angling skill, instinct and sensitivity to a subservience to technological gadgetry had begun. In the past the novice angler had learnt by the slow degrees of experience, day by day. It was slow, but not tedious - for the beginner was spellbound. When, eventually, those first little successes came, they were glorious. Now the early impact of technology brought short cuts which, shortening the path to success, progressively lessened its magic. That is the irretrievable loss. It has diluted the witchery of fishing.

Coincident with the change was what could be called the age of Richard Walker. Richard Walker was a fine angler, if great success is the criterion. Richard Walker was an engineer: he could not but apply to fishing his engineer's mind. He applied it brilliantly. But fishing is a subtle amalgam; the poet is as much involved as the technician, and the naturalist, and the philosopher. Richard Walker, the engineer, was sincerely clear that he should apply to the maximum his specialised gifts. Often it was like the turning of a clear light upon old problems, and often it was to the immediate benefit of those hungry to catch fish.

Some of his innovations, apparently small, had far-reaching effects. The Arlesey Bomb: a little thing, but how widely it has expanded the ways of legering. It is an example of the centuries-old pattern in which new and completely helpful, completely harmless perfecting is given to an ancient technique. Before

I have always felt that the simplest tackle is the best. The greater the gadgetry, the more the angler is distanced from his quarry. For this reason, I love the simplicity of a centrepin flyreel.

LEFT *The River Allen is a quiet stream, weaving through the Dorset meadows. It is long since I was there, but I remember summer days, the sound of cows cropping grass behind me, while we fished the shallow crinkle of its water over the stones. We had to crouch and creep if its trout were to be caught.*

RIGHT *This mirror carp was lent to me by the zoo. It was small, with fins large in relation to its body, as is the way of young fish. The mirror carp is a variant of the common carp, but it only has a few, greatly enlarged scales, mostly along the lateral line.*

Walker's brilliantly-simple development I, and no doubt multitudes of others, had for various rolling leger methods made a coil of lead wire stopped by a shot. It had often been successful. But, how good to have the Arlesey Bomb.

With such things he augmented our fishing days, and had matters continued thus all would have been well. The beginning of technology's real invasion was probably the first uses of electricity. To the first buzzer bite alarm much blame is to be attributed. From that point, the path has run downwards, away from the sensitive ancient delights towards the takeover of lifeless technology.

This was the time of the Carp Catchers' Club, an exciting time. By various means, mostly inspired by Walker, we were catching carp that had never before been thought catchable. I remember with tingling clarity those ink-black nights of solitary fishing by spooky pools, defending my bait bag from marauding rats. My bite detector then was the holding of the line with thumb and forefinger: it was perfectly effective. But in the course of hours skin can lose its sensitivity. I moved up to what was to be my technological limit - a fold of silver foil on the line. That worked too, excellently.

Then came the electrical bite alarm. At once

and instinctively I recoiled from it. It was introducing between me and the fish a foreign, unnatural element. It was outside the frame of nature. It was intrusive, jarring, not nearly as thrilling as the silent slipping of line through the fingers in the pitchy night. Anyway, who, properly attendant on his rod, should need such a thing?

Fishing to me then, and still today, is the moment-to-moment suspense-strung contest between the fish and me; I want to lose no moment of that. If I go fishing, I fish: if I need to sleep, bed is the place for that - or, if on the bank, then I do not want to leave a merely artificial device to do the fishing for me, so leaving out a greater part of what angling is, or should be. If a device calls me harshly to tell me it has done my fishing for me, I am the loser. I have robbed myself. Let it be said again - it cannot be said too often - fishing is worth just the pleasure it gives,

the true full angling pleasure. To fish by any means - especially if utterly unnatural, inorganic forces do the fishing for me - is not fishing as all the generations of anglers have known it.

Richard Walker, it has to be emphasised, was completely sincere in believing that all he did, guiding fishing forward, was unquestionably for the best. It is unfortunate that his way left out some ingredients not separable from the full joy of angling.

Nevertheless, fishing, left entirely to him, could have continued in reasonable health perhaps. He was a very fine angler within his code; and he was dedicated. So are his heirs dedicated; but in their unswerving following of their master they have carried his principles to the point of distortion.

A central part of the Walker code was the pursuit of very large fish - that, for him, was the primary objective. The gentle pleasures of the waterside, the be-witchment, were irrelevances. This was the business of records, beating the rest, piscatorial muscle-flexing. It was athletics, Olympic gamesmanship. Fish were the means, what the ball is to football. In the ranks of 'specimen hunters' there were, and are, many of the truest kind of anglers who have, perhaps temporarily, caught the contagion: but it must be suspected that the fully-convinced specimen hunter's creed has to exclude the gentle Waltonian ways. They would regard that as not reaching the pinnacles of angling virtue. This of

Walker's Arlesey Bomb

course is not to deny that good anglers of the old Waltonian spirit love to catch big fish - that is as proper a part as all else. All of us hope that such red-letter days shall come to us. But between the coming of them, or even if they never come, we can amply enjoy, with no sense of loss, the blissful pleasure of fishing.

Once it is accepted that to win, to catch bigger fish than all others, is the ultimate quest, other elements must be regarded as being of no consequence. All technological advances must be seized, conscripted to the cause. So the path is set towards the entire taking over by tech-nology of the old delights of fishing. It is possible to envisage a time, perhaps not so far off, when the angler's part is just to be the keeper of his tackle.

One form of 'angling', now well established, attains almost completely to that state. Carp fishing, as shown by those of the cult, is a very depressing warning. In our old - as they can now be seen to be 'classic' - days of carp fishing, we used the simplest of ways. I cannot recall that for bait I ever used anything but bread in some form: I had no need to. Allowing for the tendency of carp to become cond-itioned off a much-used bait, so leading to necessary bait experimentation, carp fishing continued to be successful by the simplest means - in the hands of good fishermen.

Now, if you can, imagine an angler formerly successful in the pursuit of carp but for a number of years out of touch with carp fishing. Imagine him, quite unprepared for what is to come, entering a tackle shop. The counter is covered by what appear to be packets of sweets of a multitude of colours and flavours. These, he now learns, are boilies. They come, packet-ready, factory-flavoured. The buyer has nothing to do but put them on the hook? No, the returning carp fisher finds, they are put on a 'hair rig' - a device by which the carp hooks itself somewhere in the region of the mouth, it does not matter where. The fish hooks itself, and without the necessity of any skill on the part of the 'angler'.

It must be said of the modern 'carp fisher' merely that he is present when his big carp is caught. He sets up his rods in their rests and connects them to the electrical bite alarms - and often there are six of these rods. They in turn are connected to - what is its name? - a monkey riser? Now, with his six boilies out, work done for the time being, the 'angler' retires to sleep. In due course the bite alarm's note wakes him; a carp has picked up one of his boilies, thus hooking itself, with no need for striking. A light glowing on the monkey riser tells him on which rod the fish is hooked. Back to work - he must pick up that rod. He is successful. Angling magazines are constantly full of photographs of these successful 'anglers', the photographs being all-but identical.

It is all so simple, so undemanding in terms of experience, skill, instinct, judgement. Small boys can do it, as can those unskilled of all ages.

Consider those boys. They are cheated boys; so young they are ruined. Not for them the long magical sequence from first novitiate to experienced angler. That joy they can never know. They will never have that sublime experience when, the very first time, a small fish, probably a bristling little perch, is drawn pulsing from the riddle of the water. These boys, the boilie boys, start by getting a monstrous carp; they have the photograph to prove it. Are they now going to wait through many endless but enchanted hours for that first small triumph? Those boys' loss is heavy; it is irretrievable.

Sometimes a man is to be found in attendance upon the tackle that is doing the fishing for him. All is fully electrified. Does he, he may be asked, fish for other fish as well as carp - roach, pike, perch, barbel? No, says he, just carp. He is a tackle-minder. Now, as I hear, fish finders -echo-sounding devices - are also widely available.

I know a very good carp angler, the best one I know. He fishes with great simplicity and great knowledge and experience. He uses no mysterious factory concoctions, no automatic devices. He has no need of them - he has skill and knowledge instead. This he has gathered, coming up from boyhood in the old lovely way. Chris Yates is, to me, a real angler. In his simple way he caught a carp far bigger than any other so far caught. He caught his 51½ lb fish on an old Mark IV Avon rod with an old Ambidex reel. A teenager, a devotee of the carp cult, said resentfully of Chris, 'But he uses old tackle'. Heresy indeed.

But when all has been said, when all condemnation of modern ways has been declared, there could be a happy marriage of what is old and what is new and helpful. Such has been the case throughout angling's history. It is the coming of synthetic materials and electricity which has brought the distress. I cannot see that electrical devices will ever be really for the good of angling.

Yet much as I love split cane, I find much happiness and helpfulness in my Hexagraph fly and

This big carp had forced its way into an eel trap on the Middlesex Colne and was awaiting my collection. I went with a suitcase filled with wet grass, and brought the fish home in it. In a glass tank I put it and made my studies over the next few days. Not wishing the fish to injure itself as I took it out of the tank, I used trout-tickling tactics until it passed into a state of trance and could be lifted out inert. It finished its life in London zoo aquarium.

spinning rods. Their carbon construction follows the same principle as split cane, and I pay sentimental tribute (and why not?) to my long love of split cane by using the deluxe version which is given a finish that copies split cane. I have some of the old feeling of split cane coupled with the completely undeniable superiority of the Hexagraph's material. In this I find a happy partnership of old and new to the sustaining of my angling happiness. It uses the benefit of innovation without lessening the need, and pleasure, of using the old knowledge, instinct, experience.

CHAPTER TWO

A Mirror on Fishing

One day in 1945 I was in the bar of the Press Club. The war was over and I was on the staff of the *Daily Express*, as I had been since 1937. I was talking to Sylvester Bolam, whom we knew as Byshe: he was Assistant Editor of the *Daily Mirror*. It was not a memorable conversation, one that ordinarily would have left no trace on the memory. Byshe, without much difficulty, was prodding me into talking about fishing. It could not have been foreseen that so unconsidered a conversation should have such considerable consequences.

On the *Daily Express* I was working as an artist and, sporadically, a writer. From time to time I wrote pieces about fishing, and I think it probable that they took some colour from my impassioned feeling for the sport. So my work there seemed likely to continue. I was content; the *Express* then had not fallen from its 1930s peak, and was stimulating to work for - and, it seemed, I stood reasonably high with the Editor. But he was away from the office for a period and I fell into a confrontation with an assistant editor. At this susceptible moment I was invited by the *Daily Mirror* to join them. That was the beginning.

But not immediately. My first responsibility was the 'dream strip'. Probably the dream strip is entirely unremembered now, though at the time it had almost a fevered following. 'Send us your dreams', readers were asked, and that, enormously, they did. From the plethora that landed on my desk I selected the more arresting and illustratable ones. I drew them in strip cartoon form, and they were published with a psychiatrist's interpretation. Its addictive appeal brought a flow of dreams which showed no sign of stopping. Why it was stopped I cannot remember. Instead I was instructed do a gardening strip.

I had always been a gardener of sorts, much inclined to the loving of flowers and shrubs and trees; but of the stuff of the allotment holder and the back garden vegetable plot I did not feel myself to be well enough informed. I asked for a script writer. He was Jack Hargreaves.

Our fictional gardener, newly into life, must bear a name. Jack Hargreaves gave him one. He called him Mr Crabtree.

It appeared at first that his life might be short; the strip languished. Mr Crabtree was given a new script writer, one who lacked Jack Hargreaves's sparkling script sense, but who had the essential earthy grasp of practical gardening. But still the strip trudged: it limped on until, in January, winter's catalepsy was on the garden.

'What can we do with Crabtree now?' they asked me.

'Couldn't he go fishing?' I suggested.

Mr Crabtree, erstwhile gardener, leaped overnight to fishing fame. He never did get back to his garden. Now I was my own script writer; nobody touched Mr Crabtree but me. I needed to do nothing but let him and his son Peter, as of their own volition, flow from me. I was they and they were me. They, in their innocent absorption by the spell of water and fishing, were none but myself.

At about this time Byshe Bolam, in whom our Press Club conversation had been gestating, sometimes asked me to write fishing pieces. The Editor of the *Mirror* had come to retirement, and his vacated chair fell to Byshe. Among his first enactments was to send for me.

'You,' he said, 'are now Angling Correspondent of the *Daily Mirror*. I don't want to see you in the office more than one day a week to deal with your letters. I don't want your copy to smell of the desk.' He also ruled that I was to be freed from the normal plague of sub-editing of writers. My work was not to be subbed; not a word to be changed.

Until then the national press had had no informed and professional coverage of angling - such as that, for example, which was given to racing. Angling journalism had not been invented. Angling had had some inconsequential attention: some papers awarded prize rods for best catches of the week or month. That, haphazardly, was all.

In Fleet Street, in those post-war years, it used often to be said that the best staff jobs in national

LEFT *Mr Crabtree began life as a gardener in my strip cartoon in the Daily Mirror. But it was difficult to keep him busy during the winter months. Eventually, I suggested that he should be allowed to go fishing and that was an instant success. Mr Crabtree became the conveyor of my fishing philosophy: his fictitious young son Peter was based on my own son.*

RIGHT *An episode from Mr Crabtree's plug fishing expedition for pike. I hope it conveys the excitement that I felt when pike fishing, the thrill of anticipation.*

journalism were self-made. Mine, with no predecessors, could not be otherwise. It was as though, like a garment, it was tossed to me before an open door beyond which lay the world of anglers, uncharted by journalism. I must scan it, distil it, so that in the *Daily Mirror* there should be all the sense and fact of it. It must be for fishermen a national voice which they could accept with respect. Angling instinct and experience must be one of the most certain of its tools.

At this distance it can be seen so analytically. At that time, as with Mr Crabtree, I did no more than be myself. I wrote my column as a sort of intimacy, as though it was a spontaneous waterside conversation. Had I been pressed for self-declaration, I would probably have seen myself as having, through the *Daily Mirror*, a trust - though at the time that would have been for me much too self-conscious a suggestion. If I had allowed myself such introspection I would have discovered in myself a cloudless belief that I was serving the brotherhood of anglers. I was fortunate in having no burden of inheritance - I was first into a fresh field.

One inheritance I did accept - that of awards for outstanding catches, though I discarded its previous ways of application. Run in such a fashion that it could have the respect of anglers, I felt it would enhance the pleasure of receiving. I wished that it should not be impersonal, that it should be a means of greater intimacy between the *Mirror* and its angling readers. I made the awards annual and in three groups - one for angling clubs, one for individuals, and one for juveniles. The last I thought specially important. I remembered my own beginnings.

I was anxious that the tackle awarded should be seen to have been chosen with knowledge and insight, and whatever sort of tackle it was, it should be the best of its kind. The Avocet was an example, a classic rod designed for the Hampshire Avon style of fishing. It was made by B. James & Son of Ealing, London. I awarded many of them; now, so long after, it is keenly sought by collectors.

Results for the first year showed plainly that with just one open competition for the whole country there could be no justice. Anglers in whatever part of the country must fish such waters as chance provided. In nature's original provision, waters were very widely varied. Those of an alkaline source bred finer fish than those not so blessed. Then upon that, man

had put his spoiling hand. The alkaline rivers, anyway superior, were the ones less afflicted with pollution. The fisher of a northern canal could feel it irrelevant to compete with the glory of the Avon of Hampshire and Wiltshire.

I devised a system of regions. For clubs, individuals and juniors, I set up three regions in order to level opportunity. Though indeed I knew that no ingenuity could be so subtle as to make unblemished justice, I sought to make as bold a step towards that as I could. It did work quite well.

The winning of an award was, I hoped, a memorable pleasure - but what more could we do, how could we create such a sense of occasion as never to be forgotten? We initiated the *Daily Mirror Angling Awards Luncheon*.

It must be remembered that this was soon after the war. The shadow of the blackout years still hung; there was still every sort of shortage. People's lives had been cramped and were now only partly relaxing. There had been so little fun. Of touch of luxury, none.

To all our winners went an invitation to a splendid lunch at the Savoy Hotel in London. Against the drably straitened background of the immediate post-war years we sought to make that luncheon as exciting and enjoyable as possible - embowered with flowers, a luxury of food, ample wine, cigars for all the men, cigarettes for the women, cognac and coffee. To introduce the panel of top table speakers there was the scarlet dignity of the Toast Master. For juvenile winners we provided rail fares for child and adult escort.

Each year I think our guests found the pleasure of it without blemish. Each year a few became most

decorously and happily drunk. The day, always a Saturday - unless memory has taken on a rose tint - was holiday-fine.

It was an off-shoot of the lunches that in the evening I should go on the air. There was then a radio programme called *In Town Tonight*. 'We stop the roar of London's traffic,' said the announcement, 'to bring you interesting people who are in town tonight.' The traffic noise fell silent and we were on the air, live.

My first time on the programme was with a couple from Hollywood. He was the current Tarzan in the cinema, she, his wife, was Arleen Dahl, a film star of some brilliance. He was immense, very tall, magnificent of shoulders, godlike of face, golden-haired, a glorious object. As though bespoke-made to match him she was ecstatically tall, and as remote, blond and beautiful as he. They were aloof, not quite credible. Also there, hardly to be noticed in the brilliance of their dazzle, was a man modestly quiet. He was Tennessee Williams.

It was for that same cause of spinning more intimate threads between the *Mirror* and its fishing readers that I travelled widely as a speaker at anglers' annual dinners, presentations and such things - a practice which was to continue long after my parting from the *Mirror*. It had wide contrasts - I always striving to be even between the great and the small,

RIGHT *Many memorable times I stalked chub on the Wye where they used to thrive vastly - perhaps they still do. They lay in the cavernous eddies against the bank, never entirely refusing to feed - bold-headed shapes idling on dusky fins. This picture is of no actual place: it is simply typical of those idyllic days on the Wye.*

the humble and the better-heeled.

I went to the annual dinner of the Red Spinners at the Trocadero at Piccadilly Circus; that was quite august. I, chief speaker at the top table, was rawly conspicuous in my herringbone tweed. I found everyone else in white tie and tails or low-cut evening gowns. I had to suggest to them that they were hiding their light as honest anglers.

I also went to the annual get-together of the Prince Albert Angling Club which had its being at the Prince Albert pub in a back-street in Leeds. It was a warm gathering; they were very good men and honest anglers. They presented me with a leather fly book of the North Country kind, gold-inscribed to me. I have it still.

I received, and maintained, an intimate web of contact by correspondence with anglers all over the country, many becoming friends of standing over the years without our ever meeting - indeed I think I knew many of those faceless friends of correspondence better than the great many I met in passing at the innumerable functions I attended. It is difficult to find any intimacy of depth in large multiple meetings. But some of my correspondents I did know well and warmly. A few I did meet, but not many. One correspondent first began to write to me when, I believe, he was not out of his teens. Throughout all the years thereafter he continued to write. When he wrote most recently he had become a pensioner.

I travelled with my tackle, for the feeding of my column. Once in the deep of darkest winter, I was at Potter Heigham by the Norfolk Broads. With a hired boat and outboard engine it was my way to go by the River Thurne to turn off into Heigham Sounds, so justly known for its pike and rudd. It was lonely there, lost in its ramparts of reeds; just water, reeds, and sky. The cold bit hard, the wind was strong. Entering one of those lay-bys that open off the main channel, I did not notice that the sub-gale was pushing me more deeply in. Though conditions were hostile I did take a pike of about 12lbs on a plug; then found that the boat and I were crammed by the wind against the ice that filled the end of the water.

I strove with the oars, pushing against the ice; but for every inch I gained the wind bullied me back before I could add more inches. It was at this time that I noted that the boat was entirely of metal: the outboard was heavy: I was alone. Nothing was to be seen but towering reeds, ice, wind-piled water. The afternoon was declining. Darkness could not be far off.

I would use the mud weight to get me off. I would throw it on its rope as far as possible, haul up on it, then flog with the oars with immediate speed. The weight was heavy; it could not be thrown far. The interval between its sinking and my hauling was short. Each time I was thrown back to grind against the ice. The light was sinking and the boat, if overturned, would have had much the same buoyancy as the weight. The circumstances stimulated effort. Eventually I did gain an extra two or three feet and in that barely sufficient interval I achieved strokes enough to claw back into the wind, then to start the engine. It was pitch black by the time I got home.

I fished with Edwin Vincent in that same week: Edwin was the son of the great Broadsman and pike fisher, Jim Vincent. Fishing Horsey Mere I heard the story of Jim's hooking the greatest pike of his life - a life filled with great pike. He had it at last rolling by the boat; his old friend, companion of many fishing days, so many of them epic, had the gaff. His were famously able hands with a gaff. The only mistake of his life he made now - he fouled the line. The fish rolled its whole great length of flank under their eyes; then slowly it sank away. They agreed that its weight was not less than 40lbs.

On that day with Edwin, the sky was wild with the voices of geese. The pike we caught were more brightly green than any I have seen elsewhere.

It became necessary when I was preparing to write *Angling Waters* that I should go on a tour for the gathering of material. It was January; my tranquil journey took me through the mild-skied levels of the country of the Great Ouse, through Suffolk and Essex, on through Kent and onward to the glory of the Hampshire Avon - then still in its undiminished loveliness. I went on to Devon, to Slapton Ley - its fame for pike and rudd still then not lessened. Turning towards home I became ill. Once home my illness seemed likely to turn to mortality. I had duodenal ulcers, matured over many years. They sometimes produced devastating haemorrhages. But I lived. The Editor, I heard later, spoke an edict: 'Bernard must not

Forty-pound pike come once in a lifetime - at best. It was Jim Vincent's profound bad luck that his rolling 'monster' never made it into the boat.

ABOVE *This was my artwork for the jacket of the re-issue of* Mr Crabtree Goes Fishing, *which resurrected the book 41 years after it first appeared as a* Mirror *publication. The net subsequently became known as a 'Crabtree net' but few anglers nowadays use them.*

RIGHT *Dace are delicate sport on the dry fly and, though never very big, have a silvery elegance.*

die,' he said. His instruction must have created some difficulty for the *Mirror* staff.

After tottering through convalescence I took a week of bliss, painting at Dedham in Constable's country. But, the Editor said, I must take a month off. I must take it idling in a lovely place of my choice. I went to Ireland.

I had been to Ireland before: immediately after the war's end I had wandered inconsequentially, going first to Ballinasloe in County Galway, an old grey town. There the River Suck runs in slow loops and has great shoals of bream. It has other fish too, but I remember the bream. It was at Ballinasloe that I first came to know that memory-haunting smell of the peat fire - or, to be Irish about it - the turf fire. There is nothing else that could so symbolise old Ireland - particularly Ireland's west. On recent visits to Ireland I have found, broadly, an absence of that soul-searching scent. That saddened me.

After Ballinasloe, my earlier wandering took me onwards to Connemara and, at last, to County Clare - County Clare, the place of the Little People, of limestone crags and water. I came to Corofin and from there found Kilnaboy. I found Loch Inchiquin and all that maze of lakes round about.

There now I returned for my month of idling. I idled energetically and with delight. I painted and fished because the stimulation for both was not to be denied and, though on sick leave, sent back copy regularly. I fished for trout in the River Fergus and for perch and rudd in the lakes. I had no hint then of what was to be the result of this idyllic pause. Ireland and its fishing had put upon me its spell. There were to be consequences.

As is the way, the best of fishing is inseparable from its context. In the Ireland that was my discovery then, there were also the people. Not far from where the Fergus has its source in the limestone crags, it runs very sweetly through Elm Vale - or Elam Vale as they say there. The trout, often with that high-coloured beauty and size which belongs to alkaline water, rose well in the evening to the BWO and the big sedges. Fishing there, going my free way, I met a man. He was quietly courteous; he conducted me, pointing out those places that consistently did well, giving me the help of intimate local knowledge.

Who was he, I asked afterwards? It was he who owned the place, farmed the land. He was quite recently out of prison. But how should a man so clearly of good intent, of such quiet charm, be so lately in prison.

'Ah sure he hit a garda,' they said. A garda is a policeman.

Once I met a garda... He stopped me as I drove into Corofin. He was official, rather severe: I had to show him my papers. He was examining them when he saw my rods in the car.

'Ah 'tis fishing y'are,' he said, absently returning my papers. 'If you go up there by Kilnaboy, sure you'll find the fishing good.' He was at pains to tell me the pools I should fish.

Phil Zec was in charge of strip features and publications at the *Mirror*. He began to talk to me about Mr Crabtree. 'Why shouldn't we make it into a book? Think about it.' That, I think, must have been quite early in 1948.

Thinking about it quickly became obsessional. Mr Crabtree had started fishing in the paper in January, going on from there with the passage of the seasons. What more reasonable structure could there be for the book, what more natural shape? Going through the year's fishing as I went myself, perhaps my own sense of the water, its smell, its air, would seep into the book. Already the as-yet-unwritten book was so real to me that I could almost touch it. I ceased to think of it as something contrived, made up, devised for public eyes to see. Mr Crabtree ceased to be a character for my reporting. We fused, he and I. He was I, I was he. When I began work on the book it emerged mainly as my own privacies. I had only to let it flow out.

I had to design the book, do its typography, paint its colour pages, but in that there was little sense of work. All were inseparable. On many a book when all else has been done, titling can be a problem: this one all but titled itself. 'What are you going to call it?,' Phil Zec asked. As if he had asked me my name I said *Mr Crabtree Goes Fishing*'. Equally, I might have said, 'I Go Fishing'. Essentially, that was the truth.

When it was done and I had received an advance copy, it happened that Jack Hargreaves dropped in. He scanned the book. 'This book,' he said, 'will sell a million.' It was nice to hear that, but I took it to be a figure of speech. 'Thanks a million,' people say.

On the day of publication, Tom Phillips, Assistant Editor, wrote in the *Mirror*. 'Bernard Venables has written and illustrated the best fishing book since *The Compleat Angler*.' All this I took to be hyperbole - the book had to be sold, hadn't it? I did not believe it. I did hope that I had produced a book which would give some pleasure.

Sales of the book were immediately huge and did not abate; they continued so year by year, rising to a million copies, then on to pass another million. It gave no sign of stopping and would, it seems, have continued thus indefinitely. But the plates for the colour printing wore out; some had gone beyond usefulness. A new edition was produced, those plates that were beyond service were taken out and the book bulked with new material. It was awful, utterly out of sympathy with the original book.

Years passed, and once when I had been long parted from the *Mirror*, I happened to pass the *Mirror* building. I saw in its window a large notice that proclaimed that *Mr Crabtree Goes Fishing* had sold well past two million copies. It seemed nothing to do with me. I had no sense of parentage. It was no more than an echo from an old, dead past. After all, I had never had a penny from it for I was a member of the *Mirror*'s salaried staff when I created the book. The Crabtree phenomenon had continued, was continuing, and I had been unaware.

From time to time middle-aged men told me that they had grown up on Crabtree. But that was all. In such ignorance I might have remained had it not been for Merlin Unwin.

He proposed that he, then with Unwin Hyman, should produce a facsimile edition of the original Mr Crabtree. The copyright lay with the *Daily Mirror*, but they, most helpfully friendly, released to us that part which relates to books as distinct from newspaper rights. It was done, I was reunited with my own book. I found myself received back into the Crabtree brotherhood of millions.

The crucian carp is not a fish to attain great size, but it is one of particular charm - or so it has always seemed to me. My own affection for it might be to do with the fact that it was the first fish I ever saw and caught. In any case, I have always found its shape curiously pleasing. This watercolour is one of my series of life-studies of British freshwater fish.

CHAPTER THREE

In the Time
of Angling Times

I first met Howard Marshall in the bar of the Savile Club. It was there, later, that he told me of his idea. Howard Marshall was then a very famous man, a broadcaster renowned for the eloquent richness of his bass voice and for his radio commentaries on Royal occasions. More importantly at this time when fame has faded, he was a devout angler of the all-round kind. He was an excellently loving trout fisher with just as warm a love for coarse fishing. Above all, he was devoted to roach; he was a good and successful roach fisherman.

He had nourished his idea; it had been a long and solitary preoccupation, before he talked of it to me. It was that there could be a place for a national weekly fishing newspaper - a tabloid newspaper, perhaps rather in the manner of the *Evening Standard*. He asked that I should dwell on the idea, consider if I might be willing to join him, so that should it come to reality I should have the editorial running of it.

It was an engaging thought; the field was open. It was only to be guessed that a potential public, not yet aware of its need, would receive it eagerly. My time on the *Daily Mirror* could be said to have invented angling journalism; this did seem to be its logical extension.

But on the *Daily Mirror* I was happy; I enjoyed a warm relationship with the multitude of our angling readers. And I was secure. It seemed indeed that I was as benevolently situated as I could reasonably hope to be. To leave, to throw in my lot with this bright but unproved project, must be a very big decision, a gambling one. Not to do so was but to settle back in my happy safety. Even now, gazing back down the years, I cannot say with certainty that I made the right decision.

I think Howard might have been more effectively persuasive than I realised at the time. His conviction carried heavy, if gentle, power. I decided that I should take the leap.

A third partner was needed - one that should provide the material essentials, finance and plant. Quite soon, Howard found him. R. P. Winfrey had the family business of East Midlands Allied Press which owned a series of local newspapers in the East Midland area. For EMAP, statically set in that mould, such a venture as this could be the means of breaking out. The decision was taken: a national fishing newspaper was to be born.

The first stages of its gestation were obscure. In a small upper room in The Strand, London, the germ had first nurturing. On all fours, on the bare boards, experimental pages were laid out. Then came promotion to one room, then to two in Breams Buildings just round the corner from the *Daily Mirror*, then still in its old home in Fetter Lane. From the Hulton Press came Colin Willock as our first Editor;

Ken Sutton was Circulation Manager, and I was Editorial Director.

After the first six months Colin Willock left us. There then came an oddity of editorship. At the behest of R. P. Winfrey, a joint working was set up: Jack Thorndike became Features Editor, Peter Tombleson News Editor. They were co-equals. It was, as it were, a horse bearing a head at each end - and, naturally, the horse found difficulty in pulling to the best effect. So much was recognised in, I think, 1957. Then Jack Thorndike became full Editor. Peter Tombleson had a roving commission.

We had Tiny Bennet, 'Mount Tiny', six foot eight inches tall, darkly bearded and grizzly-voiced, a visual asset for any infant paper. He, formerly a *Mirror* staff photographer, now became ours. His presence at angling occasions about the country was highly visible. He played to the gallery with innocent pleasure because within his great bulk there beat the heart of a child. Tiny, alas, was not reliable. The time came when, in spite of my struggle to shield him from wrath, he was dispensed with. For a time he free-lanced insecurely, then emigrated to Canada. Canada took him to her trans-Atlantic heart. His big ways had found their natural stage. Tiny quickly became a TV star of the Great Outdoors. Had the outdoors not been great, Tiny would have made it so. Then, poor Tiny, so prematurely, he died.

Reception of the news of the paper's approaching birth was mixed. Alf Waterhouse, then President of the National Federation of Anglers, declared that we would be lucky to sell three thousand copies. He was out-numbered but not alone in so thinking. We had no such uneasiness.

On 10 July 1953 *Angling Times* was born and of that first issue, 30,000 copies were sold. From that first moment its infancy was robust. It had no sales drop-back which is the normal pattern after first issue. *Angling Times* strode forward, building its circulation unfalteringly.

The leader column of that first issue bore at its top the title with the kingfisher logo which I designed for it; below that was the legend 'Founded by R. P. Winfrey, Bernard Venables, Howard Marshall.' Below that was an angling riverscape which I drew. The arrangement was that the leader should be alternately written by Howard and by me. I wrote the first one. It read thus:

'This journal which first meets the world today, 10th July 1953, is for the angler. Then who is the angler?

'Is he the Yorkshireman who catches trout and grayling and salmon, and, lower down, coarse fish, in those rivers that come down from the Pennines, over the high moors to the plain? Yes, he is the angler.

'Is he the man of Sheffield or Birmingham who goes at his weekends to fish in matches or catch his bream in Witham or Severn? Yes, he is the angler too.

'Or is he perhaps one of those who fish for flat fish or conger, sea bream or bass or any others of the fish that may be had round our long coast? Yes, he also is the angler.

'So are the men of the Thames and the Lea, the fishers of the Great Ouse and all its tributaries, those that fish the reedy maze of Norfolk waters, and all the men of Somerset waters, Brue and Parret, and Sedgemor Drain. All Britain's coarse fishermen are the angler.

'The angler is also the catcher of salmon in Wye, Dee, Deveron and Tay; the trout fisher of Test or highland burn, Teme or Tees, reservoir or loch.

The angler is everyone in whom is the love of the waterside and the bending rod.

'All this multitude, is in this, one man. Coarse fisher, trout fisher, salmon fisher, sea fisher, argue as they may within their ranks, have a common interest, a common bond. So great a throng with one purpose, whatever its differences, needs a voice to speak for it, to represent it, to inform it; it needs a common ground where all its points of view may meet.

'All this, *Angling Times* will do. It is the angler's own paper. I hope he will find it worthy of him.'

In that first *Angling Times* there was a column that for many years to come was to be informative, stimulating, so often controversial, such compulsive reading. *Dick Walker's Pitch* had begun. That first one, quietly discursive, discussed bite alarms. Dick was a convinced user of bite alarms - indeed, unless my memory is at fault, he invented them. His column established the pattern that was to follow - an undecorated directness that drove to the point.

'Perch With a Price on their Head,' said the headline on the front page, thus announcing a promotional programme designed to bring awareness that *Angling Times* had begun life. So starting at

'The angler is everyone in whom is the love of the waterside and the bending rod'

23

Kingston-on-Thames, then on about the country, perch bearing numbered tags were released by me. The first four to be re-captured thereafter were to win cash prizes - £20 for the first, £10 for the second, £5 for the third, £3 for the fourth. From the deep south to Stockton-on-Tees in the north the fish releases did create strong local attention.

First issue also saw first life for Mr Cherry; he and his young friend Jim doing week by week, in cartoon strip form, what had been done by Mr Crabtree in the *Mirror*. It cannot be pretended that they, though successful enough, ever attained the imaginative and loving hold that was the gift of Mr Crabtree.

Browsing through those long-gone early issues of *Angling Times*, I came upon that of 15 October 1953. There I find Dick Walker referring to 'a little contrivance' he had just devised for the fishing of Arlesey Lake in Bedfordshire. He had a problem in reaching the great perch that lay very deeply, and hitherto inaccessibly, in the lake. Just for that, specifically, he knocked up his 'little contrivance'. Anglers of today probably have difficulty in imagining a world which had no Arlesey Bomb. So quietly was born the indispensable. But all that has gone, for the leadless so-called Arlesey Bomb of today is a travesty.

Still browsing, I find the lead story of 9 October 1953 bears the headline: 'Venables Invited to Ireland. Ambassador of Angling.' 'Eire', runs the story, 'has invited Bernard Venables, Editorial Director of *Angling Times*, to make a goodwill fishing tour of Irish waters to report on their coarse fishing possibilities to British anglers. The tour will last nearly three weeks'.

Officials of Fogra Failte [now called Borde Failte] say:

'We believe there are fabulous fish just waiting

ABOVE *My design for the first Angling Times book which I compiled with Howard Marshall, published in 1955. The contributers included Jack Hargreaves, Dick Walker, and 'B.B.'*

RIGHT *I painted this perch for my friend Peter Rogers. We admire this species for its bold colour and fighting spirit.*

Bernard Venables

to be caught, who don't know what a float looks like. Bernard Venables will be the first angler to have received a formal national invitation. He is, in fact, the first Ambassador of Angling.'

That tour, largely through the Irish Midlands, was to have consequences which continue still. It was a quiet country that I found, little frequented, but quiet also due to economic depression. Its fishing potential had not been exaggerated. East to west across the counties south of the border the glimmer of water was seldom absent, a skein of lakes and rivers, unfished, abundantly teeming with fish. To Cavan and Clones, Carrick-on-Shannon and Cootehill, every-where I found the same promise of a coarse fishers' paradise, untouched.

I wrote a long report for the guidance of Fogra Failte; and in *Angling Times* I reported my findings over a number of weeks. Their warmth is evident still, remembered from so long ago. In my first *Angling Times* report I wrote:
'Here in the Republic of Ireland I find myself with a reversal of the English angler's problem. It is not "Where can I find fishing?", that I must ask myself but "How am I to select from such a huge range of opportunity?" I can go where I like; I need no permits, no day tickets, no licence. In every direction that I can go there are lakes and rivers that I could not exhaust if I were to fish a different one every day for years to come. They are all free, they all teem with fish. A great many of them are virgin waters so far as coarse fishing is concerned.'

My reports had their effect. The first trickle of English anglers swelled quickly to a flood: the flood has never abated, apart from a temporary slowing arising from the troubles in Northern Ireland. When,

on a subsequent visit to Ireland, I was pleased to discover that the whole economy of that part of Ireland had changed, poverty had to a large extent changed to prosperity. When fishing so good is matched by the Irish capacity for welcome, how can the visiting angler resist?

That part of fishing history, the birth of angling journalism, which had its beginning with the *Daily Mirror* probably made the coming of *Angling Times* inevitable. What has transpired from that has probably been no less inevitable. But suppose the path had not gone the way it has, suppose there had been no *Angling Times*. Angling journalism has undoubtedly influenced the sport beyond all expectation. People of the generations since mine (nearly everybody!) would barely recognise the face of angling in the former days of innocence.

Early in the life of *Angling Times* it became obvious that if the paper was to retain its circulation through the winter, readers must be persuaded that there is no reason of nature for the fishing to end in October, and that the months of winter could and should provide fishing no less worthy than that of summer. To this end, in 1954, the *Angling Times* Winter League was founded. It prospered exceed-ingly. I, no match angler, am told that the *Angling Times* Winter League story is now virtually the story of match fishing in England.

Until the birth of *Angling Times* the barbel had been a widely-desired but only narrowly accessible fish, confined to a few favoured rivers. But now, *Angling Times* learned of a riparian owner on the little River Enbourne which runs into the Kennet at Aldermaston Mill in Berkshire. He wanted to be rid of the barbel that swarmed in his water, wishing in their place to stock trout.

Angling Times, under the initiative of Ken Sutton, took out his barbel. With the agreement of Fishery Boards, the barbel - varying from 2-9lbs - were introduced into rivers that till then had no such blessing. Barbel were put into the Severn, into the Bristol Avon. In the Severn they have thrived exuberantly and hardly less in the Bristol Avon. They were also put into the Welland where they are holding, and into a few other rivers less successfully because those rivers were less suitable. Barbel now are also established in the Wye through, it may be guessed, spreading from the Severn by way of their common estuary.

In my role as ambassador for Angling Times, I had the good fortune to mingle with anglers of all ages and all levels of expertise. What united us from Belfast to Norwich was our love of fish and fishing.

My attendance at the annual occasions of angling clubs which had begun on the *Daily Mirror* intensified at *Angling Times*. My tracks left few parts unvisited and in circumstances no less varied. In Glasgow it was black tie and dinner jacket; while in Kidderminster a member sang *The Road to Mandalay* and the pints flowed till 3am, and in their warmth they presented me with a rug woven in one of the carpet mills in which many members worked.

In Norwich the Lord Mayor and his Lady were gracious at the top table and, when all seemed done, a committee member in the distillery trade brought to each of us on the top table a bottle of whisky. It seemed ambitious after the not mean drinking that had gone with the meal. But these, after all, were not events of constant occurrence - just once a year they came. For everyone else, that is, but for me, at the year's busy time, they were more like once a week.

At Nottingham, where I presented prizes for a juvenile competition, I shook the grubby, worm-tinctured hands of over 80 boys with hardly a pause, and at Belfast I sat through all the very fully-worded annual business of an angling association meeting. At Birmingham I attended, and of duty survived, a number of anglers' social occasions, and not one of them failed in hospitality. And so too at Llandysul on the River Teify, where Billy Williams, member of the Welsh International Flyfishing Team, was host of that worthy pub the *Half Moon*. Sonny Cragg, *Angling Times'* most excellent staff photographer, was with me. We left the *Half Moon* after three o'clock in the morning; Sonny and I and our host were among the few survivors.

So it went at Colchester and Canterbury, Kings Lynn and Aylesbury and many, many another place. It

was sometimes quite a stern test of endurance, but endurance was fortified by the invariable happiness of the welcome.

In the early years, we took the *Angling Times* Forums widely round the country; of those, the one I remember best was at Cardiff. Because it was in Wales, it probably left a livelier impression, but anyway it was there that first I met Terry Thomas and Lionel Sweet, who were both guest members of our panel. I need no other reason for my clear recollecion of that evening.

Each year in January we were regular with a stand at the Boat Show. As regularly, anglers thronged to us - eager-eyed boys and all the ages to old men full of ancient reminiscence. Even women too, though in the common way angling's peculiar spell seems not to fasten on them as on men. Among those rare women was Yvonne Mitchell with her husband, eager anglers both, and she a most subtle and beautifully-talented actress of television drama.

Of the boys, many came proudly wearing their Kingfisher Guild badges. The Kingfisher Guild, founded by *Angling Times* under the presidency of Professor Magri Mac Mahon, flourished exceedingly with its junior readers. Of those early members I suppose many are now middle-aged men, mellow with long years of fishing wisdom.

From the very beginning, *Angling Times* was vigorous in its support of the ACA (Anglers' Co-operative Association). I was often involved with ACA promotions, going with that formidable and convivial propagandist and fund-raiser Ralph Erskine-Hill, then ACA's Director. To Wigan we went, he and I, our angling audience there being mostly miners, dour men and unsmiling, but responsive - in that region they had grim reason enough for awareness of pollution. At the meeting's end, bluntly friendly, they said we must come with them - 'to t'pub for sup o'ale.' It was a large sup.

The bar room tapered: wide open at one end with a two-seat bench across the other. Upon that cross seat they put us, Ralph and me. I think there were 19 of them. Each claimed his right to buy a round.

There had been, till then, much confusion and little certitude about the record fish list. There was no established system for the verified acceptance of records - many of the existing records were very shakey on their plinths. There was no panel, no official body for the acceptance or rejection of claims for new records.

Then, in 1955, a very large chub was caught. Dr J. A. Cameron caught it, but with no intention so to do. He wished to catch a salmon. He was fishing the Annan in Dumfriesshire, and this unbidden chub took his lure. Its weight, wonderfully, stunningly, was 10lb 8oz. If all had been right it would have lit the life of one angler for ever. Its captor was unimpressed, he being wholly a salmon angler with no regard at all for coarse fish. Nevertheless this was, by a large margin, the biggest chub ever to have been taken by an

LEFT *This barbel was painted from a specimen which was caught from the Royalty Fishery on the Hampshire Avon, at Christchurch. I made my studies on location, then the fish was returned to the water.*

RIGHT *I painted this chub for the first issue of Creel magazine in 1963. It illustrated an article about all aspects of the species: its habitat, behaviour and sporting qualities.*

angler. The uproar it caused was remarkable.

Angling Times researched the catch with all the care the event demanded, then accepted that the fish truly did establish a new chub record. The storm broke. Correspondence was furious in condemnation or support; but preponderately condemning. And, as always in such angling debates, there was confusion between factual issues and morality. Could it be proved that the fish was caught? Was there no deception? Our investigation left no doubt as to its authenticity; there were honorably reliable witnesses of its capture and of its double weighing. Many had seen the fish.

But there was another factor, one that, south of the border in the country of the coarse fisher, was seen as most scandalous. What was done with the fish, it was asked? Was it, with full honour, restored to the water? Well - no - it was borne home, because the lady next door had several cats. With what blanched horror this news was received! But - did that lessen in any way the validity of its capture and its identification and its weighing? It did not. Yet for many, this act was an overwhelming reason for non-acceptance of the record.

Undoubtedly it was a pity that this magnificent fish should have fallen to one who, though irreproachably an honest angler, lacked the background to know what shining fortune had come to him. He was a Scot and, as Scots are, a game fisherman. He, on his side, would have been no less shocked if he could have heard roach fishermen on the Royalty Fishery of the Hampshire Avon cry with anguished disgust when an apparently good roach bite was indeed that of a salmon - 'Another bloody salmon!'

That so hot a storm had been raised by the chub's capture made it essential that *Angling Times* should be an instrument for the resolving of the record fish confusion. I wrote to Alf Waterhouse, President of the National Federation of Anglers, I wrote to *The Field*, I wrote to each body that had a practical interest in the matter. Could we not, I asked them, set up a panel, the members of which could be accepted as authoritative? I received acceptance of the idea from all.

Within a few weeks all had been done. Major Brian Halliday represented the NFA. Roy Eaton represented *The Field*; Howard Marshall became the committee's Chairman; Peter Tombleson, the *Angling Times* News Editor, was Secretary; Dr J. A. Jones of the Zoology Department of Liverpool University and a distinguished ichthyologist was a member, as was Professor Magri Mac Mahon. I represented *Angling Times*. Also on the committee was Tom Ivens, at that time well known for his writing about stillwater trout, though I cannot recall whom he represented. The Freshwater Biological Association agreed to act as consultants if need arose.

Under the management and funding of *Angling Times* the committee was launched, and named itself the British Record (Rod Caught) Fish Committee. Its meetings were held at Browns Hotel in London, with lunch followed by business. Its rules for verification were stringent, and many previously accepted records were disallowed for inadequacy of evidence (though reluctantly because almost certainly some of those were genuine). It was considered essential that the body of the fish should be produced - a provision that later was to become out of sympathy with current feeling. At the time the rule was a reasonable one by the ideas of that time, but it did become too rigidly applied for a later climate of opinion which laid much emphasis on the returning alive to the water all coarse fish. A primary case was that of Chris Yates. When he caught his magnificent carp of $51\frac{1}{2}$lb he returned it to the water; it was disallowed, though no one doubted its genuineness. Now, very properly, the record is established.

In January 1955, the great canals storm broke; and at its raging heart was *Angling Times*. The British Transport Commission in whose hands lay the net-work of canals, sought permission from Parliament to close nearly half of them. Included were seven in the West Riding of Yorkshire, Westmorland, Lancashire, Staffordshire, Worcestershire, and Norfolk. Among them were the Macclesfield Canal and the Peak Forest Canal on which the County Palatine Association had had dearly-valued fishing for more than half a century.

The threat to many thousands of coarse fishermen was dire. They stood to lose a major part of such water as they had.

The nature of canal abandonment is that,

LEFT *The roach, at its best, is among the loveliest of coarse fish. It is a shoal fish and may be found glinting, silver-flanked, in quite murky canals. Its light and playful behaviour can delight and frustrate its devotees.*

RIGHT *There is a special time for the roach fishermen which I hoped to convey in this painting. It is the first two weeks of March, the last two weeks of the season, a time when so many of the best roach are caught. It is at that time that roach are at their shining best, actively feeding at the prompting of spring's first touch.*

32

though at first fishing may improve by greater weed growth and thus greater food and cover for fish, weed becomes uncontrollable. This, in turn, encourages silting, the canal fills and eventually becomes dry. Even, it emerged, the Kennet and Avon Canal itself was threatened - that loveliest of canals, that cryst-aline water in which roach, bream, chub, perch, pike, trout, grayling, all grew to great sizes.

In the *Angling Times* of 18 February 1955 the lead story said:

'New moves in the fight to save Britain's canals have followed closely upon the *Angling Times* story of the

danger threatening our waterways. Questions have been asked in the House of Commons, and the Kennet and Avon Canal Association has held a protest meeting. As a result a writ may be issued against the British Transport Commission to make them maintain the canal - the first to be threatened with closure...

'And - on behalf of all anglers in the country - Bernard Venables, Editorial Director of *Angling Times*, has written to the Transport Minister urging him not to carry out the threatened closures.'

My letter, printed on the same page, read thus: 'In a time when the stresses of life are greater than they have ever been, any amenity which provides some relief from the general pressure is valuable; and it is for this reason that I now write appealing to you on behalf of the anglers of this country. Indeed, even if we lived in times less troubled than ours, the case I wish to put to you would still be one, I think, worthy of attention, because the needs of the spirit can be as important as physical ones.

'This case, in which anglers share an interest with cruisers and anyone who has a feeling or a need for water as a part of our landscape, refers to the future of Britain's canals. We, and those others to whom I have referred, are very greatly perturbed by the intention of the British Transport Commission to apply to Parliament during this session for sanction to abandon a number of canals.

'The inevitable consequence of abandonment is dereliction leading finally to total drying up. For great numbers of anglers this would amount to a calamity which is possibly difficult to realise for anyone not sharing their interest, but which I assure you would be real. In Lancashire, for example, where canals provide the larger part of opportunity for those who fish, their loss would mean the loss of much that gives life its colour. Men so deprived would be poorer citizens, poorer workers, men with a sense of lessened stake in society.

'You may feel that this country's anglers are too small a minority to justify so much consideration, but I submit that this is not so. The growth of angling as a governing passion is a phenomenon of our time, and its growth is so rapid that it is impossible to form an estimate of the number of its followers that remains valid for long. A long time back there were certainly a million anglers; now there may be three million anglers or even more.

'But in spite of this we might hesitate to press our claim to your attention if to do so had to be at the expense of society at large - if in fact we felt the continuance of the working of the canals not to be economic.

'As it is we are convinced otherwise. We are convinced that an expansion of the canal system would provide a means of transport that would be in some cases cheaper than rail transport and no slower; and we are also convinced that it would lighten the burden of our overcrowded roads at a lower cost for the goods being carried.

'In view of the arguments which I have put before you, may we ask that you give your most earnest consideration at least to the continued use of such canals as we still have, and better still an expansion of the system?'

Thereafter the storm increased its fury. *Angling Times* reported that in the north-west anglers and boaters had united their strengths, particularly in defence of the Macclesfield and Peak Forest canals, and had issued thousands of petition forms to be presented to Parliament. The National Federation of Anglers and the Birmingham Anglers Association had advanced, sending into the battle the might of their affiliated associations, calling upon them to lobby their MPs. Questions were asked in the House of Commons.

All through 1955 agitation increased; by the latter half of the year the canals, and particularly the stake of anglers in that matter, had become a major Parliamentary issue. The front page of *Angling Times*

on 15 July carried the following:
'CANALS PETITION WILL BE SENT TO THE QUEEN.
'Anglers who fish the Kennet and Avon Canal - threatened by the policy of the British Transport Commission - are not standing idle. They have decided to send a petition to the Queen in an effort to retain the canal as a waterway.

'This was announced at a public meeting in Devizes, called by the local branch of the Kennet and

Avon Canal Association, when it was decided - during a long meeting where feelings were strong over the threatened abandonment - to send a motion to the Prime Minister, the Minister of Transport, and Members of Parliament concerned.

'The motion read: "That this meeting considers that the government has deliberately and knowingly failed to fulfil its statutory obligations in the matter of the Kennet and Avon Canal, and demands a full and impartial enquiry into the future of the canal before any steps are taken." News of the anglers' petition to the Queen was given by Dr Bernard Hancock, President of the Devizes Angling Association, who appealed to everyone from villages along the canal to see that every adult puts his name to it.

'Speakers at the meeting included Bernard Venables, Editorial Director of *Angling Times*, who praised the excellence of the canal for the fishing, and said that more people today were turning to the sport for moral and spiritual refreshment.

'To deprive people of the canals would, in many parts of the country, deprive them of the opportunity to fish at all.'

Through the rest of 1955, through 1956, and 1957, the war rumbled on. Eventually an independent enquiry was appointed and, even more eventually, it reported. The canals were saved; at long last an in-dependent body was given authority. The Inland Waterways Board came into being. Now was all restored to happiness?

The Kennet and Avon Canal is now restored; its fallen locks are re-built, navigation once again is possible, narrow boats for purposes of leisure line its banks. All has gone full circle, and yet anglers along its tranquil miles are returned to sadness. How ironic can be the turn of history. Those emerald weed beds that sheltered such splendid roach are gone, destroyed by boat traffic. The crystalline water that compelled the polishing of angling techniques is now turgid, opaque, churned to soup by boat traffic.

Other great causes covered by *Angling Times* bore fruit more unqualifiedly sweet. Constantly *Angling Times* supported the ACA, giving front page reporting of its cases - and indeed, some were sensational enough; none more so than that against the Consett Iron and Steel Company. This was a large company, well-established, rich, employing many workers. But also it polluted the river Derwent in County Durham. The sufferers were the members of the Derwent Angling Association, people of no power or money, apparently defenceless.

Defence they had though; the ACA fought and won against the giant. The company appealed but lost and were refused permission to appeal to the House

ABOVE *I painted this oil long ago, in the 1940s. I can still remember the quiet summer afternoon on the Sussex Ouse when I began studies for the work. It was a meadowy, almost sluggish stream, but I hear that impressively big seatrout still run it.*
LEFT *A shoal of chub from the original Mr Crabtree Goes Fishing book.*

of Lords. A precedent had been set.

Looking back through *Angling Times* pages at those early years I find myself surprised by records of my own fishing. Did I really have such fishing, such good fishing, such fine catches? There is this spread of pictures of a day's rudd fishing - lovely rudd over 2lbs, from delectably willow-hung water. Where was it? Why do I not remember it?

And there are those pictures of a day's shark fishing out of Fowey in Cornwall, fishing with companions Gurney Grice and Bruce Ogden-Smith. And yes, I do remember that. A great boatful of shark, a record for a single day's catch. There were other days; fishing recalled from long ago seems so shiningly better than that of now. But its record is only of the good days; and fishing then, no doubt, was, as now, mainly a sequence of days of tranquil pleasure; that really is the true stuff of angling.

CHAPTER FOUR

Creel

As the *Daily Mirror* might be said to have made *Angling Times* inevitable, it in its turn led hardly less certainly to *Creel*. Peering down the perspective of the years, it is to be seen that threaded through the later ones there was a simmer of discontent. At first it was slight, merely a faint shadow too formless to identify. Indeed I cannot actually remember its rising to consciousness.

All appeared as happily well as could be. My gambling plunge from my *Mirror* security had been justified. *Angling Times* was an unqualified success: the experiment had come off abundantly. Latterly our circulation was 170,000.

Perhaps that was my trouble: the days of pioneering were over. The adventure was done. Now, week by week we had simply to go successfully on. I can perceive now that, though unconsciously, I was feeling confined. A large part of myself was, so to speak, out of a job. My creative self needed further employment.

I would have felt so anyway; but there was another factor. My co-founder Pat Winfrey and I were fundamentally at variance. He and I, neither being anything but honestly himself, could not but come upon each other from time to time, headlong and unyielding. His impulse was for production before all

else. I held my standards dearly. 'Get it out Bernard,' he would say, 'Get it out.' I would dig in my heels as to the quality of what I got out. He called me a perfectionist, and the way he used the word it was no compliment. His urgency made him see my stickling as obstruction. Although it seemed that we might continue indefinitely in this uneasy truce, I can see now that two forces so unable to compromise must, in the end, come to crisis.

And, unacknowledged, my own discontent was accumulating pressure. I needed something new. Unbidden ideas were revolving in my mind, as yet phantoms. Only by stretched degrees - only really after my departure from *Angling Times* - did they take on a solid form.

I had been producing the paperback books of Mr Cherry and Jim. Four had been published and were doing well - *Fishing for Roach*, *Fishing for Perch*, *Fishing for Trout*, and *Fishing for Pike*. I was working on *Fishing for Grayling*. Pat Winfrey urged me strongly to cut corners and this was not compatible with the care that to me was essential. It was a culmination. It led me to what was virtually resignation. After nine years, *Angling Times* and I had come to a parting. Sad regret and excited expectancy were mingled. I was certainly going to miss working with the editorial staff; particularly with Jack Thorndike with whom I had had a very happy relationship through his years as Editor.

But - now I was to do something else. Now those unacknowledged ideas could be identified, admitted to discussion. I knew now what I wanted to do. I wanted to create a magazine. The want, now realised, was urgent.

Not just a magazine; I wanted to create a very

good magazine, a beautiful magazine, a magazine dedicated to the highest standards. I was determined that it should be such a fishing magazine as had not been before. I wanted to show that, written in impeccable English, printed on good paper, with good design and typography, with colour, it would lose no popularity but would in fact be all the better received for that. My whole conception was based upon the warm conviction that, given the chance, the broad spectrum of anglers would respond. If this

ABOVE *There is ample reason for the cult of the tench. In its supple rotundity, it is a beautiful fish, so lacquered, so luscious. Its little crimson eye so well becomes it. This one came from Wire Mill Lake in Sussex, where I briefly lived.*

RIGHT *The day is clear and fine, the hour is early. The water, untouched by wind, reflects the trees. And here again, as wonderfully new as ever, is the fat and shining beauty of the tench.*

thing were to be done I must have complete freedom to do it in no way but my own.

About this time a new colour printing process had come, giving greater freedom of colour on all sorts of paper. It was called web offset. My magazine should be printed by web offset. So far I had no one to provide money for printing any process on any paper: but for such a venture as this, I felt the most essential need apart from inspirational urge was optimism. This I had. I did not really doubt that I would find a backer.

I prospected. I went to see Jocelyn Stevens, who had transmuted the dull old metal of *Queen* into the new glitter of *Harpers and Queen*. He was a man of lively eye and perspicacity; he showed interest. But that never hardened into an outcome.

I continued to probe here and there, and though time seemed to lengthen discouragingly, it was not long before a way was found. Max Reinhardt had recently published my book, *The Gentle Art of Angling*, and he had some sort of association with Wilfred Harvey. He arranged that we should meet. Wilfred Harvey was the Chairman of Purnell, printers and publishers. He was also Chairman of the British Printing Corporation. He was Chairman of all sorts of things. Also, he had a new web offset machine, a splendid monster of a thing: and it was currently under-employed.

He received me in his office in Mayfair. He was small, tiny indeed. His desk was large and he, behind it, sat very upright, white-haired and with eyes that seemed to be packed with sparkling blue glass chips.

Very clipped and sharp he asked me what was my proposal. But, it was clear, Max Reinhardt had briefed him well. In five minutes, I knew I had found my backer. He continued the form of questioning, sharp and darting. I told him I proposed a magazine of 64 pages, with 16 pages of full colour and 16 pages of two colour.

'No', he snapped, 'full colour all through.' I pointed out that it would be vastly expensive and would put off for a long time our breaking even.

'I don't mind - don't mind. I've done very well from the British public - feel I owe them something - social service. Don't mind if there's a loss - for the public good.'

'Nevertheless,' said my inner self, 'better to do it my way - everyone will be happier if we can reach a break-even not too far in the future.'

'Now - all right. When do we start?' The blue glitter was fastened on me. 'Have you got a car?' I had not. I had been driving a company car.

'Well - what do you want?' My mind's eye made a quick survey from Mini to Rolls and boggled.

'Here,' impatiently, calling his secretary, 'Miss Sharp' (I have forgotten her real name) 'cheque book.'

'Here,' open cheque, 'I've signed it. Get what you want. Got any money? Probably not. Cheque book, Miss Sharp.' He wrote a cheque, gave it to me; it was for more than a comfortable sum. 'Tide you over - sort things out later.'

I had been in his office half an hour. I walked out dazed. Dazed I walked up Piccadilly. Without belief I looked at the car sales rooms opposite the Ritz Hotel. Thus, in thirty minutes, my magazine was given means of birth.

I could give way to my urges. I could think of beautiful pages, the scents of fishing on paper; I could soak myself in the joy of work. Now I must think of a name for this treasured magazine that was to be born.

The naming of a magazine is no matter for haste. Many candidates must be thrown up, turned this way, that way, discarded. The obvious names must be run through to get them out of the way. It is when every easy-coming name has been pushed aside that the right one has chance of emergence.

When it comes it must be simple, easily memorable. Preferably it should be one word - one precious word. The word must convey atmosphere; in its one little package it must have the sense of the water, of bending rods, of melting air in water meadows. When at last I found that softly-charged word, *Creel*, it was already started on its way to becoming a cliché. Now, in these later days there are the signs of it. But then, it was fresh, untouched, new but with the taste of tradition. *Creel Magazine* it must be.

Creel had its birth in July 1963. Its leader column which I wrote touched a response in readers; it has often been quoted to me since. This was its first paragraph:

'Here is a new magazine; its dedication is to sanity. There is in a way an inevitability that it should be so; it is something that comes from the nature of fishermen and fishing, and this is a fishing magazine. We live in a time when we are driven to the defence of our balance, when all seems set to destruction of our reason; these are tense times, brash strident times. Artificiality, the denial of our natural roots, our proper instincts, strides over us. It is a token of our times that man, in his distress, turns to things in which he can find reassurance for his natural instinct.'

In that first issue I made large use of contributors previously unknown; from then on I built them and others up so that they became well known. A few, after one very successful appearance, made no return.

Turning those long-gone pages I find an article on fishing the upstream worm for trout during the dog days of summer. It was an excellent piece, utterly authentic. William Watmough wrote it. Who, till then, had heard of William Watmough? I found him by local grapevine in Yorkshire, and William Watmough was a devoted angler of the old Yorkshire kind who all his life had been practising such Yorkshire arts as the upstream worm. It was as though he had been called

from the water, waders still wet, and asked to explain the ways of what he was practising. He wrote no more; he was not called out of the river again.

And there was Leslie Brewer, the late Leslie Brewer, a butcher from Reading in Berkshire. His local river was the Kennet. All his life he had fished the Kennet. No one knew that subtle river better than he. He too was in the first issue, writing of Kennet barbel; it was excellent. This first issue was also what might well be called the inauguration of R. V. Righyni;

LEFT *This is a recent watercolour I made for a series of prints. September is the best month for barbel fishing. The season, and the strong flow of the river, express the true atmosphere of classic barbel fishing.*

ABOVE *These barbel are fish of the strong current, nearly flat of belly, smoothly arched above from strong head to tail. They have no need to resist the current; fast water flows over their shape and holds them comfortably to the gravel.*

but of him there is so much to tell that I shall do that elsewhere in this book.

Another first-comer was Clive Gammon, his too an advent that was to lead far. Unlike the others, it was not the compulsive love of fishing that impelled him to write. Anyway Clive would always have been a writer; he was so made. He became a very skilled professional journalist. But he was as passionate an all-round an angler as could be. His *Sea Column* was a regular feature from the first issue. In that same issue his just-published new book was reviewed: I wrote the review.

The first two paragraphs ran thus:
'Future generations of sea anglers may call Clive Gammon the man who abolished the bell. The rod-tip bell, endlessly waiting to summon its often too patient owner, symbolises much of what sea fishing has been - what it can never be again after the impact of Clive Gammon and his school. He found it crude and heavy; he seems likely to leave it an art, as much an art as freshwater fishing.

'As Mr Gammon says in the introduction of his new book, *Shore Fishing* (Macgibbon & Key, 18/-), "But the sport remained, as a friend of mine put it, a bit thick-eared, and thick-eared much of it still is". This book will do much to alter that.'

First reader reactions to *Creel* were happily encouraging - some indeed ecstatic. And, though there had been no real marketing attempt at an international circulation, response was international. Letters came from New Zealand, from Australia, from South Africa, from other distant places.

It was in this way I heard from Captain K. L. Edwards, a skipper of the Straits Steamship Company of Singapore. From time to time I heard from him, as movement of his ship allowed, and always, to me, it was a pleasure. Between his letters sometimes I thought of him, plying those magically-named seas around Malaysia and Indonesia.

I heard from Mr Poltock, farmer of Tasmania. He told me of his former days in the Cocos Islands in the Indian Ocean. He, a keen fisherman, had been enchanted by the astonishing beauty and diversity of the fish he found. As he caught them he photographed them; he bound up his collection with descriptive, typed notes into a book of his own making and binding. He sent me the book, as a gift. Clearly, the good man had treasured it. I have it still, still treasured. Its value to me is enhanced because, in later days, I was to fish so much myself in the Indian Ocean.

And I heard from America, wonderfully. Joe Godfrey wrote to me, ebullient, joyously fishing-keen Joe Godfrey: it was a major experience. I never met Joe, but our considerable correspondence led me to think him a lovable man. His first letter burst upon me thus:

'Dear Bernard Venables,
CONGRATULATIONS! Your CREEL is beautiful.

I think all creels are beautiful, but this one of yours, the Fishing Magazine, is GREAT...'

The letters continued. Joe took out a subscription. In a letter of 27 June 1964, he wrote:

'Dear Bernard,
Now back on the job ... been fishing.

We are delighted to announce to the world of fishermen for sport your election to:

THE FISHING HALL OF FAME.

Your DOLFIN AWARD, Highest Honor In Sport Fishing, is being shipped to you on July 11, 1964 ...'

The 'Dolfin Award' duly reached me. Mounted on a plaque of wood there is a ceramic dolphin. On an engraved brass plate beneath, there is the legend 'Through these portals pass the immortals'. Another letter to me announced my election as an honorary member of the Sportsmen's Club of America.

There came another letter from the President of one of the major American airlines (was it Eastern? How traitorous a thing is memory). On an airport bookstall he had happened upon a copy of *Creel*; he pronounced himself enchanted. Gratefully, he said, he found in *Creel* a freedom from fishing cliché; that it had the authentic scent of the water.

But the most treasured consequence of *Creel* in America was getting to know Arnold Gingrich, that man of eloquent scholarship, founder of *Esquire* magazine and still then its publisher. He had been for many years at the heart of cultural America, a friend of Dorothy Parker, Ernest Hemingway, Scott Fitzgerald and the rest, and himself an author and journalist, and one of America's greatest authorities on angling literature. His letter to me, first of a very long correspondence, is for me so precious that I hope I may be forgiven for quoting it in full:

'Dear Mr Venables

'For more than a decade now, I've been a great fan of yours, beginning with your book *Fishing*, in the series *British Sports Past and Present*, and culminating in *The Angler's Companion*, where the passage on the beat on the Torridge near Hatherleigh made me pack

up and go to it. That was in the spring of '59, and I hurried to get there in April, to find it as you described it. And then latterly I've been most impressed by *Creel*, and particularly by your own contributions to it.

'This admiration has now found expression, here and there, in a book I have written, which will be published by Alfred Knopf next spring, called *The Well-Tempered Angler*. In one chapter, *Salmon in Connemara and Devon*, it tells how I read your account of the Torridge and Hatherleigh and it details my own experience there, concluding "...Oh excellent author, oh venerable Venables and venerated Venables, every blessed word turned out to be true, down to the last, for no fish exceeded 14lbs. And the beat described was instantly recognisable, from the looming sight of Dartmoor down into the high-hedged hollows, past a village, past a pretty pub. Then falling twisting under a shade of trees and past stone cottages to a bridge where the water starts, the ancient narrow massive bridge patched with golden lichen hove into view ... and it was on that beat, so well portrayed in words by Venables, that the last word of his prophecy was fulfilled, for the bailiff, the

LEFT *This is an echo of that time, now long gone, when I was a devoted, almost incessant fisher of the Kennet at Hungerford. For a number of years, I had a rod on the town water. It was a very fine fishery, maintained by the late Lancelot Peart, and its anglers were a brotherhood. Doyen of us all was the late Cecil Terry, who invented those two very successful flies, Terry's Terror and The Iceberg. The latter was one of the best-ever mayfly patterns. My picture is of the millstream which runs down from Bracket Hatch to Dun Mill.*

man from the River Board, duly found us there on his "mildly admonitory round," and though he was polite and friendly, almost genial, in exchanging gossip about what fish had been taken in the previous few days, he still didn't fail to bring the conversation at last around to the point where, after a deprecatory little cough and saying "Of course you both have your licences..." and upon being assured that we did, still wondered if we "didn't mind" showing them to him. So every word that Venables wrote about Hatherleigh and the Torridge was true. How many angling books, do you suppose, would pass that test?"

Sincerely yours,
Arnold Gingrich'

That first letter and the many that followed, took us, though still unmet, to intimacy. Eventually we did meet; I went to New York. Barely had I checked into my room when the phone rang. It was Arnold welcoming me to New York, and asking if I could call round to the *Esquire* office in Madison Avenue. So began the whirl that the latter part of that day - and the beginning of the next - was to be. For all the rest of the world, Arnold's day terminated each afternoon at four o'clock when nothing would prevent him from spending a faithful evening, attendant upon his chair-bound wife Jane. But he passed me on to other hosts.

So, that evening, I found myself at the Theodore Gordon Flyfishers. It was formed honouring the name of the pioneer of the very pure dry fly tradition in America, and had among its members virtually all the most distinguished of America's fly fishermen. That evening I first met Lee Wulff, Ed Zern, Ernest Schwiebert and many others. When the business of the evening was ended I was born off to dine at a restaurant in Union Square - it then being after midnight. Quite a lot later we left there, my day, with the five hour time difference, having been a very long one through which I had floated with only a slight sense of normality. On another day Lee Wulff took me to lunch at the Anglers' Club of New York, another institution of the most stainless fly fishing purity.

Meanwhile, on *Creel* I worked very hard indeed, all seven days of the week. I had one editorial assistant, but he, schooled in a very different kind of journalism, could not adjust. So I did all. I wrote the leader, the diary, my own column, some of the book and tackle reviews, all the sub-editing, all sorts of special features: I did all the page lay-outs and typography. I wrote and drew the three-deck strip cartoon and other paintings and drawings. I could cope only by working at home, free from interference.

One day each month my assistant and the circulation and promotion manager called to collect all the matter and take it on to the works in Somerset. As the door closed on them, I began work on the next issue.

But the magazine was good, it was well received - indeed the readership was loving - so I was, so to speak, ardently content to work on. The evidence was strong that, given time, *Creel* could achieve break-even, eventually profit. All publishing experience supported that. And, had I not had the Chairman's assurance on that?

But - after three months' publication, the Chairman sent for me. He fastened me with the blue glitter of his eyes: 'We're losing money,' he said. Well, yes, of course, I thought. 'Have you no sense of profit and loss?' he said.

Thereafter such meetings recurred in parallel with *Creel*'s increasing prestige. Writing to Arnold Gingrich I must have told him of this uneasy situation, because he, answering said:
'I'm sick to think of the possibility of *Creel*'s suspension, and hope very much that your sponsor will somehow be prevailed upon to come back to his original concept of the necessary breaking-in period before breaking even. It has been such a beautiful job and by all odds the best thing on fishing produced on either side of the ocean.'

Of course the crisis came. I was summoned: summoned also were my assistant and a number of others, at least one of no connection. The purpose of the gathering appeared to be one of audience. Would I, the Chairman asked, be willing to continue as Editor if the magazine were reduced to 32 pages on inferior paper with no colour? I, knowing very well the nature of this choice (which was no choice), for form's sake asked that I might consider for 24 hours.

I was out.

I had one more issue to produce, that of December 1964. The leader I wrote for it was my farewell:
'And now here is December; it has an air of finality. The last leaves are gone; it is midwinter - or so it will be before this month is out. All the year's events, all its seasons, are gone, done now. All is over till another year shall come to be born and grow, have its spring and summer and final decline. Things come, things go, triumphs and days when fish are dour; but, perhaps, the sense of all these things is strong in me now, if you will allow me to be personal about it, for I am leaving *Creel*. My editorship is ending; this is the last issue I shall produce. Perhaps it is appropriate that December sees the parting.

'For eighteen months we have gone together, you, *Creel*, and I; and how strong the sense has been of communion through no more than a collection of printed pages. But they have been pages that have lived by the reflection they made of a passion shared, and the feeling of that has cancelled all distance, all creed, all class, everything but that consciousness of living water that never leaves a man so blessed that he is a fisherman. The sense has been strong, these eighteen months, that we are as one. There have been letters from strangers who, by writing, have ceased to be strangers - letters from all parts of Brit-ain, from Ireland, from America, from New Zealand and Africa and Singapore - oh so many places; it has been good to read those letters.

'It was July, you remember, when we started, July those eighteen months ago, when coarse fishing was two weeks old, and trout fishing was in the dog days, and the big seatrout were coming up the rivers. Thus it was in Britain, and we heard of the fishing then of other fishermen, finding their fishing in many ways in their many places. August came, and then it was September, and the trout were eager to the fly again and the deep-sea days were long with the salty

glint of sun off Cornwall and the rugged Irish coasts, and we heard of triumphs and fine days of many another coast from Florida to Kenya.

'How transitory but how recurrently permanent it seems now looking back. All sorts of things may have their time, may come, be briefly famous, go, but the delight of men in inhabited water withstands all time, all distance. Autumn came that year, and the last fine flurry of seatrout and salmon is something to remember still for the mild serenity of many days -

and a time of enchantment it was too for coarse fishermen enjoying their little season between summer and winter. Gone now, all that; but not in any real sense. As long as fish swim in clean water, that is as much present and future as it is past.

'Now another year is nearly done. Do you remember that winter here lingered on rather dourly, and while coarse fishing lost the last fine fling it may often have, we were anxious for the first of trout fishing? Such things we remember when many a portentous thing is forgotten. *Creel*, I remember saying in that first issue, is a magazine dedicated to sanity, and, through those eighteen months since, so it has been. The world in that time has been a tumultuous place; but *Creel* and its readers have had a serenity of communion that is the permanent and blissful sanity of fishing. And now goodbye.

Bernard Venables

Letters from readers mingled anger with sadness. Captain Edwards wrote from his ship, *MV*

LEFT *A salmon from the rugged west coast of Ireland. This is Barrow Harbour, a sea inlet in County Kerry and a wonderful place at low tide for watching wading birds. Across the water lies the Dingle Peninsula. Bass and seatrout also run this water.*

RIGHT *This is the Dunn at Freemen's Marsh, a minor chalkstream which runs into the Kennet. On the edge of Hungerford the parish church looks out over the reedbeds and willows. No flyfisherman will have difficulty in picturing the trout that rise under the overhang of the willows here.*

Perlis on those distant seas; thus he wrote:

'Dear Mr Venables

'I can scarcely bring myself to believe that you are leaving us. So sudden and no word of warning. *Creel* dedicated to sanity? Pshaw!

'It was too good to be true of course, too good to last. Please, Sir, I've known you for thirty years, ever since I began to read. I beg you reconsider for our, the readers', sake.

'If I had the authority you would be confined to the ship. I feel fed up now.

'Sincerely, Captain K L Edwards.

'This is a BAD BAD day

[This refers to *Creel*'s monthly competition, 'Good Day, Bad Day'. Prizes were given for the best letter describing a good day and a bad day.]

Now, I being gone, a new Editor was appointed. There was no cut to 32 pages on inferior paper; colour continued. But how dreary a thing it was, how void of virtue.

Captain Edwards wrote again:

'Dear Sir,

'I am proud to have received your letter of 20 April. I, and many others I am sure, correctly guessed the reason for your leaving *Creel* when I received the first, January's, shabby parody of your creation.

'My subscription has been cancelled.

'Sir; I am certain that I speak for thousands of fishers, to whom you have afforded delight, when I say that I await, impatiently, your return to media which will be available to me.

'In the unlikely event that I could be of the slightest assistance to you in any new project, I beg that you will find my address in the file which is nearest to hand.

'A fan, faithfully,

Capt. K. L. Edwards.

Arnold Gingrich wrote to me. 'I'm sick to hear what's become of *Creel*, of course, and I can just see the grubby thing it must be, with you and your cohorts out of there. But in a perverse nasty way, because I'm on your side, I'm also glad it's so lousy, now that they're trying to carry on without you.'

Try they did, but not successfully. The circulation plummeted. Finally, *Creel* was taken over by *Angling* magazine, and soon after it sank into oblivion.

CHAPTER FIVE

The Anglers of my Years

For so many years I have lived with anglers: I have known so many. For the better part of 50 of those years inevitably I have known most of those with at least some degree of fame. My remembrances amount almost to a biographical dictionary of fishermen. Some, famous in their time, now are hardly remembered, if at all. Some, not now among the living, should be remembered: I who knew them well, should give of them such account as I can. Some of those can stand as symbols of their time, so drastically and rapidly has the nature of fishing altered in these last 40 or 50 years.

I am one of what must be a rapidly diminishing number who knew John Eastwood - the man who conceived and founded the Anglers' Co-operative Association - the ACA. There are now a great many anglers enjoying their fishing who, but for John Eastwood, would have lost it long ago. The many victorious actions fought by the ACA have saved the fishing of a huge number of anglers. By far the greatest number of beneficiaries have been poor men whose water was polluted by offenders far too powerful financially to have been brought to justice otherwise. It was John Eastwood, a barrister, who perceived that actions under Common Law could defeat pollutors though to do so is expensive beyond the reach of any but rich individuals or groups. But by co-operation, he pointed out, the expense could be met - not co-operation between a few, but by the co-operation of the large majority of anglers working in harmony nationally. That that has been proved is now history and it is still working.

John Eastwood was also a stipendiary magistrate at Bow Street police court, and there each Wednesday a few of us waited upon him just before lunch when he came off the Bench. There was Stratton Gerrish, the brilliant solicitor who conducted those early cases; another, whose name now escapes me, who was a high official of the Forestry Commission. We were what John Eastwood called his 'inner committee'. It was our practice to go to a small restaurant nearby to talk ACA business over lunch.

About that time too I hosted an intimate lunch to introduce John Eastwood to the Editor of the *Daily Mirror*. That lunch resulted in moral and financial help for the ACA by the *Daily Mirror*. John was, as I was, a loving fisher of the Usk. After John Eastwood's most untimely death, a memorial committee was set up, with three trustees including the Marquis of Exeter and myself.

It is easy to recall my first meeting with Charles Ritz, most of 40 years ago though it is. After all I did smash his rod when we met in the Ritz Hotel in London.

But I would remember anyway; he was memorable, small, with dark eyes brittle with intelligence, restlessly observant. His hair stood stiffly as though cropped off. He was about then just starting his campaign to break into the British market with the rods of his design made by Pezon and Michel of Amboise. They were beautiful rods.

In his room at the Ritz he showed me a ten-foot salmon spinning rod; being of that classic period it was split cane, a lovely thing. It was a highly furnished room in the Ritz fashion, and, when he handed me the rod to flex to feel its action, I did not see the gold opulence of the screen behind me. I felt the sickening impact as the rod's top joint shattered - so poor a start for a new friendship. But Charles, urbanely merciful, soothed my anguish. 'We will give it a new top,' he said.

But our association survived and ripened - at least partly because Charles Ritz was a man of great shrewdness and unassertive kindness. He was cosmopolitan, and for all his years in America, utterly European. As his guest I stayed at the Paris Ritz Hotel; it was there he lived himself in a not large room close to the roof. The first night Charles and I dined in the Espadon Restaurant, and that was Charles's personal pride. The gorgeous period splendour of the hotel Charles had inherited; it was the creation of his father Cezar, lavish with mirrors and gold. The Espadon was no less gorgeous, but of later period, and gorgeous not by gold but by artful lighting.

Said Charles, 'I designed it. In particular I designed the lighting. I designed it to make all women look beautiful - even Americans.'

Espadon in French means swordfish; a stuffed swordfish hung in the Espadon Restaurant.

Across the hallway was the Espadon Bar, and that was the territory of Bertin, the barman. Having been appointed by Charles, he was of course an angler. His delight was to fish for wild carp in the Dordogne. Many an evening he told me of it, very vivid in his pleasure.

To Amboise we went, Charles and I, to visit the works of Pezon and Michel. Amboise, in the French provincial manner, lay delightfully clustered beneath the noble eminence of its chateau. There I met Pierre Creusavaut for the first time - famous Creusavaut he was then, famous as a casting champion. But is Pierre remembered now?

He was also Charles's collaborator in the designing of rods, and as we found him then he was cogitant, engrossed with the top joint of a fly rod, pacing, pausing, flexing. He was a quiet, gentle man, modest, sparing of speech. He was beloved of Charles. As in his mode of being, so he was in his casting - understated, seemingly effortless. Almost he could have seemed lackadaisical, rather as though rod and line provided their own volition. Gently he moved the rod; easily, unerringly, the line snaked out. All so easy it seemed. It was of course the perfect demonstration of the mechanics of fly casting. Pierre, as it were, conducted the tackle.

With Charles I went fishing; we went to the Risle in Normandy, a chalkstream that, by nature, was as opulently blessed as the Test itself.

In the Place Vendome just outside the hotel, Charles's car was waiting; there we were to meet. I was dressed for fishing. Charles was shocked. But no; he said, I must wear proper clothes, and bring my fishing clothes with me. There would be luncheon. That was the first surprise. The second was Charles's driving; his driving was famous and was thought to be best avoided.

'Forgive me,' he said, 'if we do not converse as

I drive. I must concentrate.' My attention became no less concentrated. He was certainly a good driver - but at aeronautical speeds.

I, used to chalkstream fishing huts, was surprised by the fishing room. It was attached to our host's house and was equipped for every conceivable fishing purpose. We changed into fishing clothes, then went back into the car and to the river, and that was

ABOVE *Not the wild, common carp of the Dordogne so loved by Bertin, barman at the Ritz, but a leather carp. This is a variant of the common species, and with the same capability for massive growth. This living specimen was lent to me by London Zoo. The painting is another in the series of freshwater fish that I studied from life. Each species I depicted head-on and from the side. They have been a marvellous source of reference for me over the years.*

my third surprise. The gravel was shaved, no sway of ranunculus, no verdant trails in the current.

We were starkly visible across the river's width. When against probability I hooked a fish it was close in under the far bank.

Charles, I noted, concentrated on lies deeply shielded by overhangs of willow. He was very adroit in the doing of it, line and fly flicking in and out like the tongue of an adder. I was told of how, recently, our hostess, an accomplished flyfisher, had taken a trout of 2lbs. It was to be seen that this was a notable event. I thought of the great trout of the Test. How equally the Risle could yield such fish if it were allowed to keep some of its weed beds for the harbouring of trout food.

We broke that day for lunch, and a break it was indeed, back to the fishing room, out of fishing clothes, into 'proper' clothes, then into the dining room to join a luncheon party under the dignified ordinance of the butler.

By Charles's invitation - and it could have been by no one else's - I became a member of the International Fario Club. Charles ran the IFC as a total but benign dictatorship. He invented it, largely he financed it. Membership had but one duty. In November each year attendance was required at the annual banquet at the Ritz Hotel in Paris. For that splendid meal, devised by a world master cook, Charles himself, only a token charge was made. The club, said Charles, was for the world's foremost flyfishers: it was true that flyfishermen of that calibre were more likely to be members. But shrewd Charles had another interest. He was concerned for the marketing of the rods which bore his name. He had sound commercial reasons that they should be well received

in Britain as their very high quality deserved. So a flyfisherman who also carried substantial editorial influence - such as I - would find his flyfishing credentials not too strictly examined.

And indeed the rods were exceedingly good, very sweet in the hand, very precise in their delivery of the fly. Charles presented me with one, the Type Lambiotte, having its name from that M. Lambiotte who was a founder member of the IFC. I have that rod still, retired, but treasured.

I, though early, was not quite a founder member. At my first attendance one very large round table was able to seat us all. It was intimate then. In later years it grew, so to speak, beyond its strength; it lost its sense of intimate exclusiveness. It grew to a very long top table with legs.

At my earlier attendances there was from England one other member. I had known Frank Sawyer before, he and I having met at angling occasions, and having done television programmes together.

Frank Sawyer was the arch-wizard of the Upper Avon in Wiltshire. At Netheravon he had been born and there lived all his life. Only in quite early boyhood had he not been on the river. Through those Avon eyes he saw all rivers - indeed all nature. He had a very considerable authority on chalkstream water and chalkstream trout and grayling. When Howard Marshall had sought Frank's advice on his Lambourn water in Berkshire, Frank, needing a specimen, had walked into the river, picked out a trout by hand, and bore it to the bank.

He was a self-taught naturalist: his college had been always the river bank as he went his keeping ways. That had taught him much, an immensity of water meadow lore, but it in some

ways a little restricted the range of his learning - he had not been able to look beyond the fences of his own learning. He and I once were talking of eels. He, with great positiveness, denied that migrating eels would cross land in conditions of rain or heavy dew. Why was he so certain? I asked. 'I have never seen it,' said Frank Sawyer. (I have seen it.)

But he took his stand most firmly on riverside trees. I - as it were - stubbed my foot on that once. We were by the river at Netheravon where a willow of great loveliness hung its boughs to the water. 'How lovely,' I said, 'and how fine a lie for a trout.'

Frank, sad of face, worried, 'It's bad, I'd have that tree out. And all the others.' I was never entirely sure what so disturbed Frank, but I think it was a belief that trees deplete river water. He was seriously unhappy.

To Frank's memory we must allow his foibles.

He was a prince of river keepers and, broadly, in day-to-day terms, a good naturalist.

In later years of the IFC another member from England was Major Oliver Kite - Olly Kite - he too was an excellent angler and naturalist. But, here was the rub, like Frank Sawyer he was an authority on nymphs and the fishing of nymphs: and he and Frank lived opposite each other in Netheravon.

They did not get on. For years Frank had had no competitor in television and written fame on the subject of the nymph. He was the heir of Skues, a high priest. Now came Olly, also highly regarded. Certainly so by Charles Ritz. I got on well with both. It was very easy to understand the feelings of Frank. He, born a simple countryman, had eventually come to international distinction in his field.

The early days of *Angling Times* introduced me

to two other great fishermen, outstanding flyfishers both, both casters of international distinction. When *Angling Times* took our *Fishermen's Forum* to Cardiff, it was most proper that on our panel there should be these two outstanding Welshmen. Thus they entered my life, to considerable consequence. The evening was delightful, our Welsh audience lively in response in their Welsh fashion.

With Terry Thomas I became a constant fishing partner. A few miles upstream of that smiling and very pictuesque little fishing town of Usk, Terry had a beat on the lovely river of the same name. It has dear associations for me. Sometimes I would pick up Terry at Redditch where he was manager of the tackle firm of Milward. Sometimes he drove himself down that route so well known to us which passed through Worcestershire and Monmouthshire; then we would meet in a pleasant pub in Raglan.

On arriving at Usk, what was our priority? With no question we must call upon Lionel Sweet at the fishing tackle shop kept by Molly Sweet, where she tied the best Usk flies. And quite often we would go across to that wonderfully flavoursome pub, *The Three Salmons*, that gazed peacefully at the world across the square. Then Terry and I would journey on to our lodgings at our well-loved *Chain Bridge Inn* that backed onto the river.

Terry's water, the Llan, lay at the end of a leafy twist of minor roads through the hills until, dropping down a track, we were into the deep secrecy of the river. Countless days of untouched peaceful fishing we had there, seldom seeing a soul until, as the light sank, there would be the excitement of inducing frantic rises by skating a big sedge fly imitation.

Occasionally Lionel Sweet would drop in on us

to demonstrate his hardly believable casting with the Aerial reel and a salmon spinning rod. With some lightning dexterity I never could follow, in mid-cast he changed hands. With an ounce lead, standing well back from the river, he would cast cleanly over the river and far up the drop of field on the other side. Lionel was one of the finest of fishers for salmon and trout, not a sort of athelte as some champion casters can be, but a true water-haunting angler.

On occasions, coming alone to the Usk, I would stay overnight with Lionel and Molly. After breakfast, as a ritual, he and I would go into the tilted field above the house there to cast with his 17-foot tournament fly rod, a mighty instrument. I, elated by having thrown 40 yards, would see Lionel reduce that to insignificance. Lionel Sweet was a lovely man; Molly matched him.

Terry Thomas was for me a fishing companion of a kind to be delighted in. But he was not popular: there were many who disliked him with intensity. I cannot deny that at times I saw reasons for that. But I must record as I found. We enjoyed our mutual fishing dearly. Terry had a wonderful sense of humour; we found much to laugh about; there by the lovely Usk we had no thought beyond. We enjoyed our

RIGHT *How nostalgia stirs here! This is the little River Clun that runs its hidden way through Shropshire. There we used to go, Terry Thomas and I, never to see another human soul all day long. The trout were not big but they were all wild. It was not easy fishing. For every fish that showed accessibly in open pools, a dozen would tempt hazardous casting under the hang of alder and willow. It was idyllic fishing. This watercolour of Terry is typical of my paintings in those days when I used less colour than I do now.*

pints and our pubs and we enjoyed our bottle of wine. Unhappily, in the end that was the undoing of Terry; but that was after those days of our fishing together. As I knew him he was a prodigiously good caster with fly or spinning rod, an excellent angler, a vintage fishing companion.

Often we talked of anglers we had known, or knew, and always that led to Terry's telling particularly of one man, so exceptional a fisherman, so exceptional a man. Reg Righyni was his name. Then it happened that both Terry and I were invited to attend as speakers at the annual dinner of the Bradford Waltonians. Righyni, a Bradford man, was a member. Thus I met him. There are few such first meetings.

R. V. Righyni was a large man, physically large, but this sense of size went further. His impact was at first overpowering. He held his opinions forcefully; there was nothing about which he had no opinion.

On the morning following the dinner we three went over the Pennines to Cumbria to fish his beat on the Lune. We were driven by Reg in his Bristol: then, or any other time, it was always a Bristol. Reg was didactically positive that no other car at all could remotely approach the virtue of a Bristol. At that time he could have had what he liked; his wool-broking business brought him an amply large income.

Over the narrow twisting roads of the Pennines we went as few could have done and lived: Reg drove as he did everything, with inspired competence. He talked as he drove, cigarette in left hand, right hand on wheel. His left hand was needed for the emphasising of his points. The points poured upon us. Thus I was first made aware of the 'Oxygen Theory'. It was to become odd to me that there had ever been a time before the Oxygen Theory.

Reg's Lune beat was near Kirkby Lonsdale, and, then, it was a very productive beat. On that day salmon were teasingly evident, showing everywhere but with no taste for what we offered. They jumped a lot, a poor sign, not that pulse-stirring slow head-and-tail roll. Anyway I was so numbed by first experience of Reg Righyni that I had little usefulness.

On the return drive and through the evening we discussed the Oxygen Theory, as we did on many subsequent meetings. I became convinced. I, with Terry, persuaded Reg to write a book. The book was written. Reg had not written before; I helped him with technical matters of writing - and indeed sub-edited the book - in such a way I hope that Reg's highly characteristic touch should not be lost. I found him a publisher (MacDonald) and in 1965 *Salmon Taking Times* was published.

The basis of the theory is that there is an optimum level of oxygen in the water which will induce in salmon an impulse to take a lure. At too low a level they tend to a depressed inactivity; at too high a level they retire to less oxygenated places. The optimum may come from a convergence which is variable with the time of year, weather and humidity. According to the theory it is possible to foresee when that benign convergence shall come. Some salmon fishermen of great experience deny that such foresight is possible. I can but say that on a number of different occasions I have seen Reg do so - sometimes quite dramatically.

The book also had a section on the mechanics of river flow and its bearing on the behaviour and movements of salmon - the choice of resting place, the paths followed when the fish are running. This section too is to some extent contrary to tradition. The book declares that logical reading of the current's behaviour, and that related to the Oxygen Theory, makes it possible to discern where salmon will lie on a strange river. The traditional belief is that only local knowledge can provide answers.

The section on salmon fly patterns is as searchingly original. Reg Righyni indeed was one of those rare people - in fishing as in other things - who could regard all the problems involved as if he was the first person ever to have done so, being in no way clouded in vision by accepted wisdom The result was often suddenly revealing and helpful.

In Reg Righyni's case it sometimes produced results bizarre in the eyes of others. Reg was confident in arguing his case, that the theory of gravity is at fault. Air pressure, he said, is the real phenomenon. Reg (often with justice) had enormous certainty of opinion. Once, Arthur Oglesby told me, he was seatrout fishing; the fishing was good. At every cast he hooked and landed a fish. Then along came Reg, and for a time he watched. 'Arthur,' he said 'you're doing it wrong.'

He was a kind and generous man, a good friend, a warm man. He is, with Charles Ritz, on my shortlist of famous anglers whom I have most respected, whatever his idiosyncrasies.

Reg's face to the world was that of a blunt

down-to-earth Yorkshireman, but his background was exotic, and indeed more closely related to the real man than that plain exterior suggested. His father was French; and he was also a Hungarian landowner. In addition, he was a linguist of brilliance. In the first World War Reg's father was a secret agent for the British on the German General Staff.

There came a time when the Germans rumbled him, and he had to make the hastiest of departures. He turned up in Paris, but there the Germans were still hotly on his trail. He was whisked away by the British, and they, for a screen, took from him his true name (which I never knew), and from the air plucked

ABOVE *The grayling, a member of the salmon family, and one of Reg's favourite fish. North country grayling tend to have rather more pointed dorsal fins than the rounded, banner-like ones of their southern bretheren, like this one from the Test.*

RIGHT *This is the Newton water on the Lune in Cumbria, which for many years was in the hands of Reg Righyni until he died. Many times I fished with him there, by day for salmon, by night for seatrout, stumbling blindly among the stones to the tail of the pool you see here.*

a name, one that belonged to no particular language. They called him Righyni.

He reached Dover knowing no word of English, but, by means known to none but himself, got to Birmingham. There, he knew, there was a language school, and English he must learn as soon as possible. In Birmingham he wandered, seeking the school. In the street he intercepted two women: a mother and daughter. They took him to the school and left him there, but not before he had gained a name and address from them. Three weeks later he wrote to the daughter in good English proposing marriage. She was to become Reg's mother. Reg was a poor linguist. Those who knew Reg as well as Terry Thomas and I did were much more aware of the French in him than of the English. He had a French mind.

In one way it is a natural step from Reg Righyni to Richard Walker - different men though they were in many ways. Both they, and Charles Ritz, had the gift of being able to regard a problem as if they were the first to have done so, however hackneyed that problem might be. It was on the *Daily Mirror* that first awareness of Walker came to me. I received a letter, closely written in a small neat hand on foolscap sheets - a number of sheets. It was an arresting letter; mainly as I recall, it was about carp fishing. Carp fishing till then had been something almost of mysticism, a story of gliding enormities below the surface, far too fey for mere mortal fishermen ever to catch. That letter, at a single stroke, made the carp a fish that was attainable.

More letters followed; we met and the meeting increased my interest. He was impressive, very impressive, but it was in a slightly odd way. His complete originality was overwhelming; but what was that within his originality? Was it a suggestion of immaturity? A sense of something like that is sometimes to be sensed in those who have a total and brilliantly dedicated concentration on one subject. It also seemed to me that there was - perhaps - a slight coldness?

Anyway, all that surely was irrelevant. Here was a person of great and original potential: I felt it to be essential that I should do anything I was able so that the potential should be realised. 'You,' I said to Richard Walker, 'should be in the front rank of angling writers. I shall make it my business to put you there.'

He had it in mind to write a book about fishing in stillwater. It was clear that it could be a memorable book. I urged him on. I introduced him to James McGibbon of the publishing house of McGibbon & Key; I persuaded him that this would be the definitive book on its subject. So came the gestation and birth of *Stillwater Angling* by Richard Walker. During production I acted as consultant to James McGibbon.

At one point he sent me a sequence in which the author declared that fishing must be approached in the spirit of the Elizabethan adventurers - going forth with high purpose, against any odds, and with total determination - or words to that effect. What, asked James, did I think of that?

'It's nonsense,' I said.

'That's what I thought,' said James.

But, freed from that, the book was good on history; it was compulsively stimulating; it was original. It had all those qualities which separate significant fishing books from the rest. *Stillwater Angling* can be seen now to have been a turning point: coarse fishing has never been the same since. When I was preparing for the launch of *Angling Times* I asked Dick Walker if he would care to do a regular column. 'It's what I've always wanted,' he

said. So was born *Dick Walker's Pitch*.

The effects of that column have been enormous. It bred a new kind of young angler, very technically-minded, and, certainly, it brought to many such success as would not otherwise have been theirs. But, just as certainly, it led to what might be called the athletics approach - a striving for resounding success for its own sake, a departure from the contemplative, Waltonian mode of fishing.

It brought to birth the 'Specimen Hunters' cult,

and that is something not comfortably at peace with the true meadowy delights of fishing that have come down the centuries. Nevertheless, it must be said that those Dick Walker columns were consistently and uniquely good; there had not been their like before, nor likely to be in the future.

I browsed back through them recently - how simply, directly, logically they dealt with angling problems, dispelling non-essentials, distilling simple answers. They were technical only, an infectious creed to which the young particularly succumbed. 'Dick Walker has no soul' it was sometimes said, perhaps not without reason. But those columns did enormously increase the success of a multitude. Dick Walker has left a mark on fishing which will remain. But he was not truly an angler of the Waltonian kind. Fred Taylor, so constant a fishing consort of Dick Walker, has written of him:

'Did he not say once of carp fishing that, "You've got to be deadly"? Did he not write that an intense feud should exist between the angler and the fish and did he not quote Kipling's "calculated craftsmanship that camps alone before the angry rifle pit or shell hole and cleanly and methodically wipes out every soul in it" as the correct attitude to develop when seeking to catch big fish?'

We differed, Dick and I, about fundamental attitudes. I extolled the pleasures of skills such as those belonging to the centre-pin reel, of casting a fluent fly line - those being inseparable from the whole pleasure of fishing. For me the pleasure that fishing gives is its only value.

No, Dick considered, fishing is simply about catching fish, the biggest possible fish: and all of those ancillary pleasures of mine were irrelevances.

The fish are there; we must get them out. How harsh a loss of fishing's happiness that seems to me.

In the most complete and reassuring contrast there was another meeting. On a bitter day in November 1955 I was on Lough Na Fooey in the wild Joyce's Country that lies westwards beyond Lough Corrib and Lough Mask, lost in the wilderness of bog and mountain there. Through that darkling day as I fished, Martin Coyne who gillied for me had told me of the clergyman who came day by day over the mountains to fish, sometimes for only half an hour. As the day's light sank to evening and the keel grated on the stones, I flexed cold-numbed limbs and slowly began to climb to the road.

I saw, as though coming to meet me, a tall man, darkly clad. Then we met; he was a clergyman. He had the quiet eyes of those who live in far places. 'Mr Venables, I presume,' he said, holding out his hand, 'my name is Alston.'

There came no immediate realisation. Then, as he talked he made a passing reference to rudd. Then it flashed upon me: but could so strange a thing be? Could probability stretch so far? In this far forgotten place? But he it was, that legendary Reverend E. C. Alston, he who until that day in July 1933 had been a country parson known only to his parishioners in his quiet Norfolk parish.

On that day he caught a rudd which weighed $4\frac{1}{2}$ lbs, a new record so far ahead of all previous sizes that there was little chance of its being bettered. But, a few days later, from that same pool he took another of $4\frac{1}{4}$ lbs, and that too exceeded all previous records. Neither fish has been approached since. Then, still in that same month in that same pool, he took two tench; they both weighed 7lbs, so doubly establishing

a new record, and one which stood for many years.

That astonishing sequence became and was to remain an entry in the record lists - 'caught by the Rev. E. C. Alston' - so, year after year, the Reverend Alston had remained a legend, still, it was to be

ABOVE *Barrow Harbour, Co. Kerry: like much of Ireland's west coast, a moody and lovely place, where the weather is fickle, changing from clear skies to mantelling cloud and back again in minutes.*

supposed, going his quiet ways in that Norfolk parish. Now, so improbably, in this Celtic wilderness, this was he. It seemed to augment the legend rather than to diminish it.

Mr Alston said he lived about 20 miles away over the mountains, in Connemara. Would I care to go there with him , to see his stuffed fish? Following his tail lights through the craggy twists over the mountains, we dropped down to Leenane at the head of that long arm of sea which is Killary Bay, then on under the high peaks and half-seen lakes till we came to his house standing above a plunge of darkness. 'The sea lies there,' said Mr Alston.

In the house he fumbled with matches to light oil lamps. 'Only for three years in all my time have I had the blessing of electricity. So much have I lived in lonely places.' As the light gathered I saw cases of fish covering the walls; and there, among them, I saw that classic brace, the two rudd, 4½ lbs and 4¼ lbs, legend made substance. And the tench too, two great fish in a company of great fish. There were great pike, roach, perch, trout, a cased company of trophies, evidence of a fishing life that, however quiet, had been phenomenally eventful. There, in the midst, was even a burbot.

Mr Alston, a shooting man too, had a collection of guns there, surely one which would hardly be bettered, spanning guns of all the years back to the eighteenth century. He showed me, lovingly, a genuine Joe Manton, that master gunmaker of the eighteenth century, an elegant thing, silver inlaid.

We had supper with Mr Alston (Sonny Cragg, *Angling Times* photographer and ardent angler, was with me). Then out to the black night, to thread the tortuous and long road over the mountains, past Na Fooey, past Lough Mask and Lough Corrib, all the way back to Cong. The astonishing evening had done little to dispel the mist of legend about the Reverend E. C. Alston.

I have already recalled some unforgettable, outstanding and happy fishing companions: there was also Dermot Wilson with whom I was no less happy. There was a period when with Dermot I fished a lot. With Terry Thomas I fished particularly on his own Welsh Usk; with Reg Righyni on his Yorkshire Wharfe and his Cumbrian Lune. With Dermot I fished chalkstream water.

That could hardly have been otherwise; Dermot was as if by nature a chalkstream fisher, and he was as good a chalkstream fisherman as ever I fished with, or was likely to. But fishing skill is but one part, and not necessarily essential, in the making of a nicely fitting fishing partnership.

The days with Dermot were light with pleasure and easy with humour shared. We fished the Itchen sometimes, sometimes the Test; most memorably we fished the tiny River Alre, that head stream feeder of the Itchen. Much of it was just a few feet across, sometimes widening almost to be measured in yards. So small, it twisted almost secretly through the fields, mischievously boggy in the high marginal growth. But its trout were big. Where the water sneaked through a culvert under the railway branch line, Dermot, deftly backhand casting, took a trout that weighed 7lb 2oz. Unclouded days of happy fishing those were. I have known none more so.

In a similar way I remember Colonel Crow though he and I never fished together. But we were often by the water together, he then being bailiff of the Somerley water on the Avon where, at the time,

I had a salmon rod. He was a most admirable friend to all anglers, a benign custodian of the water, a warm man, a fine salmon angler himself. The pleasure of Colonel Crow was inseparable from the pleasure of the fishing there.

I never fished with Ken Morritt; I was never by the water with him; but I am sure that he too would have been the best of fishing company. Is Ken, a maker of all those inexpensive but amply good reels, remembered still? He should be: he enhanced the fishing of many thousands of anglers. He was just simply and obviously a very nice man.

There is one other of whom I must tell, probably the most quietly, modestly brilliant man it has been my happiness to know. In the early days of *Angling Times* I sought someone qualified to be that newspaper's biological correspondent.

In 1946 Penguin had published a book called *Fishlore*; its author was A. F. Magri Mac Mahon. The nature of the book was such anyway as to make me curious as to its author: he was obviously not of the common kind. I sensed a learned, quizzical mind, a

very good mind. Now, it seemed possible, here might be the man I sought. I arranged a meeting; so it was that I met Professor A. F. Magri Mac Mahon - Sandy Mac Mahon. Sandy, of course, was a fisherman; he was also a distinguished linguist and an equally distinguished biologist. He was as wisely rich in knowledge of geology, of botany, and of entomology and ichthyology.

He never ceased to surprise me with fresh revelations of his enormous versatility. And, as if by the way, he was a mountaineer and a sailor. He had studied at various English and European universities, and from them emerged with a D.Litt.

He was half Irish, half Italian and had a professorship at one of the Italian universities. He had plenty of justification for pride, but was totally free of any such thing. In fact he was self-abnegating and unassuming to a fault - the fault being that that denied him the recognition and prosperity that should have been his.

As well as all this he was an excellent broadcaster and, when I first knew him, much involved with the BBC's World Service - far from profitably. He lived in poverty. When *Angling Times* founded the Kingfisher Guild for its junior readers, Sandy was its President. On *Creel* he contributed a regular feature - *What to See*, month by month telling of flora and

LEFT *The trout is in the net, safely landed. I am able to say with fair certainty that it will be upwards of 1lb, for I know that water well and have caught many of its trout. It is the Salisbury Avon, Frank Sawyer's river, here near its Wiltshire source and running gently. In mood it is a very different river from its famous lower reaches in Hampshire.*

fauna in both freshwater and saltwater. The feature was finely illustrated by that very distinguished natural history painter, Arthur Smith.

Eventually Sandy, who was no lover of the modern world and wishing no more of it, decided to retire to Ireland, there to live peacefully ekeing out his minute means. To make his choice of place he took a bicycle and rode through Ireland until he should happen upon that place and, knowing it, settle there. He found Kinsale. It was a blessed choice. As he found it, as I first knew it, the world of our time had hardly touched it. It lay round the inner harbour with an air of quiet elegance. Sandy found for himself a small 18th century house at Summercove, an outlier of Kinsale. There he lived tranquilly until he died.

At Kinsale there was Tom White too. Tom White was no native of Ireland, but where else should Tom have lived but Kinsale? For one thing alone Tom lived. Tom was a bass fisherman. Bass were his life and Kinsale at that time was superb for bass. Tom White was English; such of his speech that could be followed had the sound of London.

He was a veteran of the first Great War: he had been bayonetted in the face and left appallingly scarred and his speech distorted. It was my good fortune to be introduced to Kinsale's bass fishing by Tom; none but he knew it with such fine intimacy. The truly lovely bass fishing was in the harbour - the harbour is extensive, the inner harbour and the outer harbour, and all of it then had good fishing. But it was in the intimate ravel of tidal runs in the outer harbour that there was the beautiful fishing for bass.

It was these tidal runs that Tom White knew as no one else knew them. In Tom's care they could be followed with almost pinpoint closeness, so that all the fishing could be done with quite light spinning. It was the best bass fishing I ever had - or, as things are today, ever shall have.

Now it is past and gone, as good bass fishing is in many places where once it was fine. And Tom White, poor Tom White, he has gone too. How sad a passing of what can never be again.

There have been other anglers that I shall not forget, though I never knew their names or whence they came. I was in Morocco, fishing a lake in the Riff mountains in the territory of the notorious Riff tribesmen. I was fishing for the species of barbel that the lake had. I had been fishing for some hours, thinking myself alone. Then hearing a faint sound I

turned. There, sitting behind me was a young man, a Riff, wholly of the Riff kind, very wild-looking. In his waist band, as is the way of his kind, he was stuffed with weapons. He smiled, indicated that he too liked to fish. We were brothers. Until the time for my going came, so we stayed. When I left I gave him some hooks. I never saw him again.

And I remember those anglers of the Zambezi River. Starting at the river's source, I had made my way down all that part of the river that runs through Zambia. Now I was at my journey's end, at the last few feet of Zambia where the Luangwa River runs into the Zambezi as it runs into Mozambique. There the anglers were; three black Africans were silently fishing. They made room for me. They told me where the best fish lay, and how by casting to a certain place, I could let the bait roll with the current to the optimum spot. So we sat, fishing in comfortable companionship, hardly talking. I gave them hooks too when I left.

'There have been other anglers I shall not forget...'

Fish Remembered

For various reasons, fish may be specially remembered. I remember sharply my first tiny roach and crucian carp, both very privately memorable fish. Even the most uneventful fishing lives must store some such personal treasures. But some fish become famous - sometimes for size, sometimes for the dramatic circumstances of their taking.

There was a time, now long ago, when I fell into an obsession with great shark. Perhaps the sense of such things had always been in me, though unacknowledged. I think a taste for adventure beyond the normal horizons of life had always itched in me. That that should become attached to fishing just awaited a stimulus. Cornwall gave the stimulus.

In the 1950s, shark fishing had come to Cornwall. To a great many people it came as a revelation, a slightly shaking one, that in those familiar holiday waters there could be shark. As was to be seen, they teemed. Blue shark were the majority; but there were thresher shark, porbeagle shark, mako shark. I went to Cornwall, at first to Looe, afterwards to Polruan, then to Falmouth. I caught many shark. In that there was great initial excitement; but its first flush spent, it emerged that this was really quite minor game - only a few were over a hundred pounds; the majority were much less.

But awareness of shark had taken hold, the sense that about shark there was something which edged upon the uncanny. Especially in the blue shark this was to be felt. They were so coldly, silently, detachedly ferocious. Normally, animal ferocity is hot - the snarling fury of the leopard, the lion's earth-shaking voice.

Blue shark coming about the boat seemed so evilly effortless; they seemed to have no need of muscle, sliding rather than swimming. They were most beautiful blue on the back, milky white on the belly - their elegance seemed to enhance their menace. The lion's eye is hotly angry: the eye of the blue shark is still, cold, unnervingly hostile. The awareness of such things remains when the first spice of adventure has been spent. But if consciousness of this queer threat is to be felt in these quite small shark, what must be the enormity of it in the imponderable monsters that haunt warmer seas than ours? Thinking of that, the obsession took hold of me.

In my mind's eye I saw them, in the blue depths of their tropical waters - too far distant to be within my reach. As obsession does, it fed upon itself: find these monsters I must, if only to end their haunting.

But surely, I thought, there must be nearer places where the biological circumstances have no significant difference. Why should there not be European seas rich enough to support fish hugely big? I became absorbed in the theoretical scanning of nearer seas; I began what might be called a course of biological dead-reckoning. It led finally to Madeira.

It was soon apparent that waters holding fish follow the same general principles, whether fresh or salt. Why should I not apply to the hugeness of the sea the principles of the relatively small freshwaters?

In the Atlantic, as I now perceived, there is an abyss, an immense depth created in earth's adolescence. Down the Atlantic, north to south, volcanic furies have thrown up heights and carved out that awesome depth. On its lip in mid-Atlantic lie the Azores; to its eastern shore there is Portugal and North Africa; in the south Madeira. The Gulf Stream, that great ocean current, originates in the Carribean and sweeps north-east across the North Atlantic becoming the North Atlantic Drift. Its warm water, meeting Europe's western coast, bifurcates, one arm going northward to bring a temperate climate. The other turns south, past Portugal and Gibralter and down to Madeira. There it meets the Canary Current.

The Canary Current is cold. When a warm current meets a cold current there is an eruptive burst of plankton life. Where planktonic life is rich, so is all other life: plankton is the base of the pyramid of life in water. At the pyramid's top are the oceanic monsters. Where, more probably, should my fearsome giant shark be? Madeira, surely, should breed such monsters as obsessed me.

In England's January winter of 1959 I sailed for Madeira. Six days later I found it, a dazzling cone of life alone in the vast blue plain of the Atlantic. Its air was scented, its blossom torrential. The steep slopes culminated in its extinct volcanic crater. I contemplated the vast sea, deep blue and inscrutable; but I thought that I read it. Here there must be, if anywhere in all the world's seas, an immense shark.

Ah no, they all told me; shark there are in Madeiran waters, many shark, infestations of them, but only up to about 300lbs. My conviction was not shaken. It could not be biologically possible that there were no very big shark. In such faith I began

to fish: facing that huge expanse of water, great faith was essential.

The first fact to assault my faith was scale. My approach, my tactics, were based on Cornish experience. Cornwall's sea, within Europe's continental shelf, is shallow; 40 fathoms there is deep. Drifting in a boat, laying a scent trail, is intimate fishing by the scale of what I found now.

Madeira is an extinct volcano, thrown up from the far black depths. The winds and tides of the centuries have carved out littoral shallows from the flanks of the cone. But in Madeira even the shallows are 300 fathoms deep. They end at the chasm's lip. From that edge the sea plunges awesomely to a thousand fathoms, two thousand fathoms. It has a name, that brink; translated from Portuguese, it is the Noisy Sea. Within that daunting vastness I must find my monster.

I had to start from zero. None had gone before me. In what I sought I was that vast enigma's first explorer. There had been fishing for what might be called the surface fishes - for tuna of various species, for marlin and others. There was no pool of experience to make for me a starting point. And I had only ten days in which to turn theory into fact. Five of those precious days were to be lost by big seas. To anyone not buoyed by the optimism of obsession it would have been hopeless.

But, as may always be found by fishermen in strange waters, I had the warm advantage of the unlimited goodwill of the local anglers. They were of the angling club *O Estoleiro*. And there was Dr Ribeiro, the only big game angler in Madeira. It was he who told me of the Noisy Sea, of how it is there that the commercial fishermen of Madeira find their concentrations of fish. The Noisy Sea is indeed what in other places is called the drop-off, invariably the optimum place to fish.

That was the first piece for my jigsaw. The second was the whale factory. In Madeira then, as also in the Azores, there still survived the small open-boat whale fishery. To the whale factory at the village of Machico the killed whales were taken. Waste matter, blood and offal, went into the sea. What more obvious place could there be for the finding of a scenting, foraging, hungry shark?

At Madeira's western end there is Ponto do Pargo: there, Dr Ribeiro told me, there are great concourses of hammerhead shark. They are small, he

ABOVE *The houting is one of the so-called whitefish, a member of the family salmonidae. It bears the adipose fin which shows it to be a relative of the salmon and trout. Houting used to run up from the sea into some of the eastern-flowing rivers, such as the Kentish Stour. Perhaps they still do: but I have heard no news of it from some time. For this painting, I was forced to depend on a dead specimen sent to me from Sweden!*

said, but who knows, among them there might be a monster. There if you start precisely under the lighthouse, a long drift can be made over the shark. Also, members of *O Estoleiro* told me, there were the Desertas, 20 miles offshore, a little group of island peaks, uninhabited. The fishing there had been proved rich; shark there must be, perhaps big ones.

This then was the sum of what must be my starting point, that and the universal fact that shark, picking up a scent, will follow it to its source.

Those frail advantages were, as I was soon to discover by degrees, offset by what was almost the burden of my Cornish experience. The shark I had known in Cornwall's shallow seas were, in relative terms, fish of the surface waters. How little relation they had to such fish as lived in the black plunge of water here! I went haltingly, feeling my way from stage to stage.

In Cornwall we had drifted, laying our rubby-dubby trail, and so, in our 25 fathoms we had found the shark. Here, right under the awesome sheer of Madeira's precipices, in the profound depth of the inshore shallows, I would do the same. Nowhere was more obviously the right place to do that than close in to the whale factory. In the fishing launch *Altair* we went to Machico, to the whale factory, but started three miles out, allowing for the long drift of scent there must be there. It seemed an obvious place, but I was over-confident. Having no response we moved in, and so continued until we were under the whale factory - all this time with the bait at 25 fathoms. So the hours passed, idling in the swell until it was evening. I had still to grasp the significance of the depths. I had heard of the Noisy Sea but had not grasped the dimension. I was puzzled, disappointed.

Next day we went in *Altair* westwards under the heights to Ponto Do Pargo, still befogged by Cornwall into thinking in a two dimensional way, still not mentally plumbing those appalling depths. So far we had been searching the island's southern side, protected from the northerly winds. At Ponto Do Pargo, following directions, we started a drift directly

under the lighthouse. But there, no longer in the southern lee, the assault of the north wind caught us. We rolled and pitched at the mercy of the towering crests of the swell. We had to run for shelter. Again evening found us with no shark. I was puzzled but not in the least lessened in my certainty.

The next day I went with Avalino Camara, a member of the *O Estoleiro* club, to the fish market. There I saw the fish of the abyss. I saw that long eel-like fish, the espada, a strange creature with huge jaws and fangs: I heard of the fantastic depths at which it was taken - a thousand fathoms and more. Now, at last, I began to perceive the other element, the enormous plunge of depth.

The next day, with Avalino Camara, we went to the Desertas. This is a queer archipelago, peaks of island thrown up volcanically and looking as though the hot thrust has hardly cooled, as if molten flow of rock has barely become still. The swell broke in huge white lace on the red upthrusts, and swirled in the channels between. In those channels the members of *O Estoleiro* have rich fishing for bottom fish such as pargo. It was to be assumed that shark would be marauding there too. With a scent trail we drifted there and, soon enough, had a shark. But it was a mere 50-pounder: no encouragement.

But, said Avelino, they catch the fish there in the summer: this was winter with the air temperature probably a mere 70 or so degrees. During winter, he said, the fish go deep. Now at last I began really to comprehend the sense of that. Now it was plain - only in some black profundity within the Noisy Sea would I find my monster.

The next day I went straight out from the harbour, as all the commercial fishermen do, to that plunging edge.

A mile out I began to fish. 'Further, further,' called the fishermen riding the swell, 'Out until you see Machico beyond the point.' Then we would be over the Noisy Sea. But there, when we reached it, still all was abortive. So strong was the current that no amount of lead could take the bait down: the tackle streamed out little below the surface. So again we waited out the useless hours.

But I fell to talking to Fernando and Orlando, crewmen of *Altair*. They talked of the espada fishermen, of the almost incomprehensible depths at which they found the fish - and, often, there they found other fish: tuna, swordfish, shark. Now, in this soft and sunny air, I realised that it must be in the blackest depths below us that I should search. This was the last link; here was the key factor. By the merest chance the next day brought that which locked everything together.

The day was Sunday; on Sunday we could not go to sea. In the morning Avelino came urgently. At Machico he said, a great fish, a shark, had been taken on a handline. To Machico we went: on the beach lay the fish. It was a shark and of a kind I had not seen before. It was fearsome, about 400lbs. In its lower jaw the teeth were long and serrated, those of the upper jaw conical. Here was the last step. Those who had taken the fish told me it was out from the whale factory they had caught it, but deep down, on the Noisy Sea. So - I had been right about the whale factory; I had just left out the depth factor.

Now, on the eve of my last day, here was the end. I had no doubt now, tomorrow I would catch my monster. In the morning with those who had caught the shark on the beach as guides, I would go out from Machico. This evening I would give to the devising of tackle.

Two things were clear - if I were to put adequate weight above the trace, the trace would ride up; it would foul the line. If the weight were to be adequate it could not be lead. It must be bigger, heavier, than any lead I had. It must be expendable. It must be a stone. Basalt, a very prevalent stone there, would be ideal - very dense and heavy.

My traces were steel cable, 560lbs breaking strain, and in three links with swivels between. To the first swivel up from the hook I tied a fathom's length of quite low breaking-strain nylon; to that I would tie the lump of basalt. On the bottom link of the trace I would put a large piece of cork. On the shark's taking the bait, and on the strike, the nylon would part. Now I waited for the next day that - I was confident - would give me my awful quarry.

The day, the last day, came fine but with a threat of the torrential rain that comes often, in such winter as Madeira has. Under the precipices we steamed to Machico where the man and two lads waited to take us to our mark. At first, being out too far, we moved in to about a mile off Machico and its whale factory. A bigger sea had begun to run; the sky lowered. The drama had begun.

My tackle, which had seemed heavy, now threatened with its lightness. But it was good, sturdy beyond its weight. On the eight-inch Hardy Fortuna reel I had 600 yards of 120lb breaking-strain braided terylene line. The rod was the Hardy No 5 Saltwater, split cane. The bait was a foot's length of squid topped off with half-a-dozen sardines.

Now, almost with a sense of ceremony added to that of adventure, I lowered the bait and the great stone over the side. Now at last there should be success. But at once it was clear that, heavy as the stone was, it could not take the bait down. In the power of the current, stone, trace and all streamed out, not sinking. It would not plumb. It would not do so from *Altair*'s deck.

Now as the sky darkened and the swell grew, it became clear what must be the remedy. We put back into Machico to tow out a boat about ten or twelve feet long. In its stern was some decking and in that a small square opening. In that I would sit with my tackle: the man and the two lads would row to hold the boat against the drift, so making it possible to get the bait down.

Soon, back on the mark, all was set. Cast off from *Altair*, we lay in the lift and fall of the swell. If and when I hooked my shark *Altair* could be called up; I, with hooked fish and rod, would get aboard. From the fighting chair I would play the fish. It sounded so plausible that I half believed it.

And, yes, now I could get down. The line peeled from the reel, down, down, diminishing threateningly. Then, softly, far below, there was the touch on bottom: 500 of my 600 yards of line were out.

I only had to wait for a few minutes. There it was. A pluck faint but heavy; another pluck; a minute's wait. Then a heavy draw and I had struck. Now there was the full vast weight, a monstrous force as though it was the earth itself that wrenched my shoulders. *Altair* was signalled and came up bucketing in the swell. To scale a launch's freeboard from a dinghy in a rolling sea is anyway something for agility. Now I was attached to that enormous power surging distantly below. I do not know by what means, but I who had been in the dinghy was aboard *Altair*: I was in the fighting chair - in the chair and fighting beyond imaginable capacity, striving to pump, to lift the fish, to get even one turn of line back on the reel.

Then it was gone. No power now. Sickened, I wound the long slow wind. Now here was the trace. The steel wire of 560lbs breaking strain was bitten through as if it was a wisp of wool. It had taken just a few minutes.

Then with a new trace I was back in the dinghy. The sea was growing: the rain came, vertical rods of rain. It passed and came again. Now I had 550 yards of line out - just 50 yards left on the reel. For an hour we rolled, concurrently the rain bludgeoned us.

ABOVE *Fish remembered are not only the large ones. The delight of trout fishing is often in inverse ratio to the scale of the river. This is what Arthur Ransome called 'fishing in Lilliput'. My painting is an imaginary scene, an English idyll, in stark contrast to my other fishing memories - of those days of fear and tension on the high seas of Madeira, struggling with shark.*

Then - yes - the same soft powerful pluck. I had struck, the immense drag of force threatening to take my arms from my shoulders. The fish moved slowly, an inexorable force stealing line against any power that I had in answer. I must not yield line. *Altair* was coming.

The shark lunged away with uncontrollable power. It jerked the rod; jammed it against my leg as I sat in the hole. My leg was immovable. I twisted, dragged, striving to free it, to turn the rod. The distant force dragged. My leg must break, seemed already breaking. Then, frantically, I had freed it. With what volition I did not know, dreamlike I was aboard, in the fighting chair. Someone had helped me, taking the rod as I got aboard, thus disqualifying any record that might have been claimed. Someone was struggling to push through the bolting pin which secured the butt of the rod in the gimbal.

Now all was without shape, dimension, time; all was hazily endless but pierced with sudden stabs of memory. The rain returned and returned, we lurched and rolled in the freshening swell. It seemed that there had always been this great pain of struggle, would never be anything but it. I was locked to the distant monster. It pulled me half out of the chair; I eased off the drag making a high whine. Through all the continuance the thread was the same - not a yard of line must I yield if possibly I could keep it. I must fight for inches, strive to put back feet on the reel. I pumped, leaning back almost to the horizontal, gaining a foot or two, losing it, tightening the drag to maximum, easing it to save myself, putting frantic thrust of legs against the gunwale. But the force would not be denied.

Now I could not remember ever having started

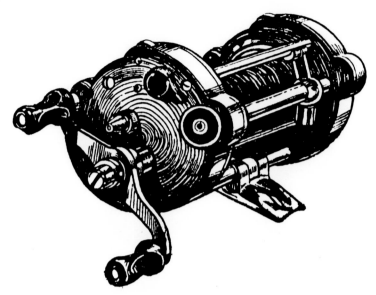

this; it could never stop. There could be no future but fighting this shark.

There came a change, almost suddenly touching consciousness. The thought came that there could be an end. The reel still seemed appallingly empty of line; there was fire in the muscles of arms and back, searing pain. The plunges of the shark, the sullen heave of the sea, had thrown me heavily, often, against the arms of the fighting chair. No part of me seemed whole. But - there was change. I had, I suppose, lifted the shark enough for change of pressure to be having effect. It put back strength into my battered being.

A moment came, engraved on my memory, vastly unexpected. Thirty yards from the boat a knot emerged from the sea. That was the knot of the double, that length of line doubled for extra strength immediately above the trace. Then - beyond belief - there was the top swivel of the trace. Then there was that moment, etched with awfulness and wonder. The sea opened; the head of the shark emerged, awesomely. How was I to believe the head could be that width? And that strangely large eye, emerald green. It seemed to stare into mine. The shark now was rolling in the surface, thrashing. As I was told, from hooking till then had been two hours. But this was not the end. There was to be another hour.

Then the shark was drawn to the boat, the gaff went in. A rope bounded the enormous girth. In the midst of the wild excitement aboard, I lay back in the chair, exhausted.

I was tired, passively triumphant in the tumult. Soon, coming into Machico, I recovered, elation being a powerful tonic. On the quay the whole population had turned out; ship-to-shore radio had told the tale. Small dark men swarmed in the boat, countless hands shook mine. The men, about 40 of them, manned the rope and, singing, heaved the shark up the quay's stone steps until it could be slid into *Altair*'s well. As we steamed back to Funchal there was a festival aboard, brandy was produced and drunk. At Funchal there was a great throng. The quayside crane lifted the shark from *Altair*'s well, and put it on a truck. To the public weighbridge both were taken and weighed. The shark was returned to the quay, the truck returned to the weighbridge for separate weighing. The difference was 700 kilos - the weight of the shark. The front page headline of *Angling Times*, 13 January 1959, read: 'Bernard Venables's 1,500lb shark, biggest ever caught in Europe.'

The figure 1,500lb was an off-the-cuff guess. In fact 700 kilos is about 1,540lb. And, in the first frenzied minutes when the shark had been brought alongside and roped, the crew had gone wild with what weapons were to hand - a giant screwdriver, a bread knife, my sheath knife, plunging and stabbing. Between that and weighing there had been about five hours of loss of blood and body fluid. That shark's precise weight can never be known: it could not have been less than 1,600lb; it was probably more like 1,700lb.

When all was over I learnt that I need not have lost heart at seeing so much space still left on the reel. The line was so compacted on the spool that it had the touch of stone. *The biggest shark ever caught in Europe*, the story had said; that was all we knew then. To the best of my knowledge, it was the biggest fish ever caught on rod and line in the Northern Hemisphere. And, it seems, it still is. It was a six-gilled shark, *Hexanchus griseus*. The Portuguese call it *albafar*.

By any standard that was a great fish, almost certainly the greatest my life will show; but greatness in fish is relative. The thrill of great catches may be as great in restricted categories as in almost unlimited ones. In the oceans there are shark far bigger than my own monster. But should a five-inch minnow be so much less a prize? I have never seen such a giant and can hardly expect to. But once, salmon fishing on the Torridge I did see in clear shallow water of sharp definition a shoal of gudgeon each fully nine inches long. I have never again seen such goliaths and

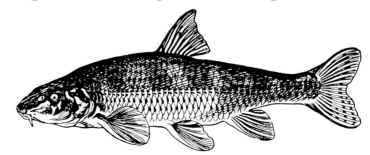

cannot explain how they came to be. Many will say I hallucinated. I am entirely satisfied that I did see them, and was in full possession of mind and senses.

One giant that came to me was surprising but not difficult to believe. It was mayfly time; the festival was in full glory. I was fishing at Hungerford. It was

12 June and the morning was lovely. Fishing at the tail of the island below Denford Mill, I had a rise of the firm kind, solid, an announcement it seemed of a good trout. My offered fly was accepted at once. With no great struggle the fish came to the net; but no trout was this. It was a dace; it was the biggest dace I have ever seen.

Beyond dispute it was a great fish. It weighed 1lb 8oz and some drams more. My spring balance could not deal in such niceties. I cannot swear how many were its drams over 1lb 8oz. It was certainly not less than equal to the dace record; probably it was a shade more: probably it was the biggest dace ever

ABOVE *A burbot would certainly qualify as a 'fish remembered' if I caught one today. There was a time when this curious freshwater member of the cod family was common in England's eastern-flowing rivers. It is now many years since I have heard of one being caught, leaving doubt as to its continuing survival there. For this picture, I was grateful to receive a specimen, sent to me from Sweden - dead of course. I had to draw on my experience of living fish to restore its semblance of life.*

LEFT *On days of early summer like this, when the flies are hatching and the trout begin to rise, life is wonderful.*

caught. But four days remained before the opening of the coarse fishing season. It was what the late Patrick Chalmers called 'a Dead Sea apple.'

In my pride I sent the glorious corpse to the Zoology Department of Liverpool University. They, surely, would be overjoyed to receive this magnificence. I received a letter from a scientific lady there. 'The fish you sent,' the letter said, 'is a dace, *Leuciscus leuciscus*.' I should have kept my monster, immortalised it in a glass case, for all generations to see.

That giant was at least a seen giant. I had to do with a giant I never saw, a fish that in its dark ferocity brought me to my knees. I was fishing at Looe in Cornwall. I was fishing for conger - but perhaps I should quote what I wrote in *Angling Times* about that day in 1956:

'A dark sombre forbidding fish the conger is, with a kind of dark fascination. Never before had I encountered it until I was at Looe this time, and my first encounter was an intense uncompleted drama.

'I, with Gurney Grice and son Julian, was in the boat *Paula* with skipper Jack Butters. The day had been good; I had had several conger, the best of them rather less than 40lbs. Then: it was towards the end of the day I met the monster. I had felt that plucking again, just a gentle plucking, with no hint that the fish that made it was 20lbs, 60lbs, or any other weight.

'As the line was plucked away, I stripped off more from the reel, giving the fish all the time and line it wanted. Then it went solid.

'I had the sense from that solidity that this was something different. Either that, or that other sense that we anglers say we have, told me that here I had something on my hands, something almost inconceivable.

'I put the rod butt in the harness bucket, clipped the harness to the reel, raised the rod gently to feel what was there. Through the tightening line I felt that I was hooked to the Equator.

'I struck; something vast below me rolled, as if the ocean itself was rolling.

'Now I strained furiously to the rod, fighting so that the huge unseen slowly-lashing creature should not find its purchase on the rock before I could raise it clear. The rod that, so far, had never been more than slightly bent to any shark, now doubled over painfully.

'I had no sense of time now, only of that awful striving force below which rolled and turned so slowly. I leaned further and further back on the heaving deck, striving to counteract the force that dragged at my shoulders. "If this is a record," I heard Jack say, "someone is going to be drunk tonight, and it might be me."

'Now, incredibly, I was on my knees. For the first time in my life I had met a fish that could bring me to my knees. But I was confident, still confident. I would get it, I thought, and it would be a record.

'Then the fish gained the rock, and became so solidly locked that I might as well try to lift the rock itself as dislodge that fish.

'I could go on to tell all I tried to bring it free, but why prolong so tragic a story? The end of it was that the hook came back. I had lost this giant conger.

'But the next day was another day, and how better to spend it than to go back to that rock? Perhaps this king of congers would take again. The extraordinary thing was that it did.

'This time I was determined that come what

Days spent sea fishing with Jack Butters off the Cornish coast were always full of surprises. Perhaps it is this constant sense of the unknown, the mixture of wonder and trepidation at what will emerge from the depths, that makes sea angling so compelling. Here we are examining that leaping fighter and frequent companion of the mackerel shoals, the garfish.

may it should come up, and as soon as I felt its rolling weight I fought with cracking shoulders to raise it, gaining a turn of the line at a time. And, slowly, with vast and tortuous slowness, it began to come, turn by turn.

'Jack, at my shoulder, said "It's coming me love, it's really coming," and, presently, I had gained about 15 feet of line.

'Then, heavily, irresistibly, without my losing a turn on the reel, just by stretch of the monofilament line, it sounded again and became fast on the rock. Again, after a time I had the hook back clean.

'Presently, astonishingly, it was on again; and again the same savage exhausting fight was on. But after a time of which I have no count, all was suddenly slack, and I wound to the surface - a large pouting, about two-and-a-half pounds!

'In its mouth was bait and hook. Laughter broke out in the boat, then stopped as we saw that the pouting was dead, deeply bitten from end to end. We looked at each other and wondered what was the great maw that had engulfed that fish. That was not the end, as you might have expected it to be. Even once again my bait was taken, and again there was the same enormous struggle. Only the end was different. This time, on some sharp edge of rock, the line was severed. That *was* the end. On the following day the weather was too rough for us to reach the rock.'

How similar that account, written at the time, is to the one I gave just now of my fight with the great shark. The circumstances were different, the scale otherwise; all is relative. The great dace, the gudgeon seen, were in English rural peace. The other two were linked by their naked savagery: but for the fish, in their own respective underwater worlds, it is the same original jungle.

But another story which rises from memory must certainly be seen in that same context. Its setting was not in the slightest less raw or wild. It was in Zambia, on the Zambezi River and on that part of the river which is known as the Zambezi Valley, uninhabited country. The little tsetse fly keeps man away - that fly, small as it is, for sheer savagery can compare with anything. The same could indeed be said of the Zambezi River itself. In its richness of life it includes both the tigerfish, ferocity unbounded, and the great vundu. The vundu is a catfish, but one which often attains an almost frightening enormity. I had heard much of it, of its huge surge of power. They told me it would twitch apart 80lb line like wool. It haunts the Zambezi through much of its course, but it seemed more fitting to me that I should seek it in this wild place where man was scarce and great beasts abundant.

At this part of the river there is an island a few miles long, on its one side the river's great width, on the other a channel between it and, so to speak, the mainland. At the downstream end of the island, hippo dwell in their wallowing concourses. Their vast sighs and grunts drift on the air much as the voices of cattle do by homely English rivers. Their place is about 300 yards out from the mainland bank where I came to fish. I had with me the cook from the Game Department camp, and John Kabemba of the Bemba tribe. There I had come with the determination to catch the legendry vundu.

'If you hook one,' they had said, 'don't try to stop it. Let it run - let it finish its first run before you try to do anything. Use really strong tackle.' Mine, I thought, was not strong by the standard of what they told me, not 80lb line, merely 30lb; but I thought it should do. My hooks were large, the bait was steak from the camp kitchen.

The scene was stimulating, very suggestive of dramatic events. The great backwater below the island seethed. Tigerfish surged and slashed, swirling as they chased prey in such a way as I never saw except at this one place. But I was not concerned with tigerfish; I baited and cast that I might take a vundu. I had not long to wait for a bite.

Almost at once the line was whipped away; but only briefly. The monofilament line fell slack, severed, at once. Mere monofilament could not withstand the fearful fangs of tigerfish. Tiger seized the bait before the vundu could approach it. So they did each time I cast with new hook and bait. I had been rather lavish with the giving of hooks on my way down the river: soon, the tigerfish had cleaned me out of what remained.

'That's it,' I said to John Kabemba, 'no hooks left. Finished.'

Said John, 'My friend, you must have another hook.'

'No John, I have not, not one.'

'But my friend, look in your bag - there must be another hook.'

I looked in my bag. There was nothing; just one tiny spoon bait with a tiny treble hook, and on a short wire trace of 7lb breaking strain.

'There,' said John, 'there is another hook.'

Absurd of course - such a fragile trifle for attempting to hook the enormous vundu. But John was insistent; I must try it.

On its little hook I put a trifle of steak bait -

ABOVE *Not the conger but the common eel. This live specimen was given to me by the London Zoo aquarium. Having painted it, and wishing it to have its freedom, I took my eel one wet day to a field near the bank of the River Cuckmere in Sussex. I wanted to put to the test the theory that eels, when on their spawning migration to the Sargasso Sea, will cross land in wet conditions to reach a river running to the sea. I noticed that its eye was enlarged and its body silvering a litte, typical indications that an eel is ready for its sea journey. I put it down on the soaking grass, and with no hesitation it traversed the 100 yards or so to the river and slipped in. I hope it reached its sea destination without mishap.*

'When you strike, you must strike hard!'

about the size of my little finger nail. All was so slight that on a 30lb line I could flip it out only a few feet. At least it was too little to gain the attention of tigerfish. For a few minutes it lay, unbothered.

Then, slowly, quietly, line began to slide away. It did not stop; it slid and slid, the reel gently emptying. On the reel I had 300 yards; soon I saw the spool through the coils. Then it stopped. It had gone as far as where the hippo wallowed.

'Now you will bring it back,' John said. On that wisp of tackle? But, tentatively, gently I felt through rod and line. That which was at the line's end yielded, began to come. Heart-in-mouth, softly, I began to wind. Still it came. I reeled in with my finger tips. I must make no jerk, no betraying worrying at the fish. Perhaps - perhaps, it could be.

Over my shoulder I called, 'John, do you know how to use a gaff?'

'My friend, what is a gaff?'

'That stick with a steel hook at the end - there, on the ground.'

Out of the corner of my eye I saw John pick up the gaff. Alarmingly, he flexed his arms, swelled his barrel chest.

'And what must I do with this gaff?'

'If I do bring in the fish I want you to land it with the gaff. When I give you the word, reach out over the fish's back - just smoothly, easily, pull the hook into the back - no swiping, no slashing - just calmly. Then pull the fish ashore.'

'I understand my friend.'

Still the fish was coming, line gathering on the reel; just gently I was towing it, minute by minute, conscious of the tiny treble and 7lb trace. One surge, one heavy shake would be enough. I could not allow

myself to believe it, but landing was now possible.

Then at last, there it was; I could see it. It was a shaking spectacle. Its yellowish sepia face was broad as a flattened full moon, its barbels more than a foot long. Its little eyes seemed to regard me speculatively. It was 2-3 yards out. 'John - are you ready - gently now, no slashing.'

The fish was only feet out.

'Now John!'

By my ear there passed a hiss. The gaff came down like a vengeful judgement. Within a second the sepia mass was on the bank, something like a hundred pounds of it. John put his hand and arm on my shoulder.

'My friend,' he said, 'when you strike you must strike hard.'

These three roach demonstrate how variable that species may be, according to where it lives. These are the deep, strong-shouldered kind that chalkstreams breed. How different from the slim, longer fish of many poorer rivers.

CHAPTER SEVEN

Adventure

When I was very young, a grubby boy, my head was full of thoughts of distant places. What was I going to be when I grew up? asked indulgent adults. I always said with certainty that I was going to be an artist and a writer, and that I would be a naturalist and of course I would go fishing. But always, too, I had to add that I was going to be an explorer.

From quite early I was drawing and painting and, a little later, I did begin to write. As to being a naturalist, witness to that were matchboxes of caterpillars and beetles which rather alarmed my unprepared mother when she came upon them. I grew up, on the way passing through the art school that trained me to be a professional artist. Then I *was* a professional artist and, quite soon, a journalist too. Early certainties were justified.

But those misty visions of far places did not cease to stir. I dreamed of adventuring, of mountains and forests and great rivers; of jungles and African wildernesses. Even thinking of going beyond our own close frontiers was tormentingly exciting. I remember that, oddly, I was fascinated by the idea of frontiers and river sources - and so indeed I still am.

Pilgrimage to river sources began in a way very modest by my later standards; but deeply thrilling then. Even that had to wait: it was many years before that I found the first meadow seepage that was the beginning of the Avon of Wiltshire and Hampshire. I followed that till it found the sea.

Serious travel, true tropical discovery, had to wait far longer; not till I was in my fifties did it begin. It began then because I had for many years been bending my working life in that direction. At last I did find the mountains, the great rivers, the jungles, the African wilderness. I did gain at least a little of the adventure I had craved as a boy. I did walk in uninhabited wilderness feeding myself and those with me by what I could shoot. I did realise some of those *Boys Own Paper* dreams.

Most particularly I came to Africa, and there at last to the great Zambezi River. I saw it at Katima Mulilo where the witch doctor had saved the women. Below the village they had come day by day to do their laundering: often the crocodiles took them. Crocodiles swarmed, creeping into the shallows to snatch the women. So the witch doctor came and by the water he made his medicines. Never again, for 100 yards upstream and 100 yards downstream, was a crocodile seen.

It was a scientist, a biologist, who told me of that. Was it true? I asked. 'True all right,' he said, 'I don't attempt to account for it. Scientific spectacles can rather blind you in looking at these things.'

Upstream from there the river raged; its mile-and-a-half of width surged in great rapids. In the turmoil of the water I used to catch the steel-burnished tigerfish. Going downstream on the other bank there was the town of Sesheke: the river flows there majestically between distant banks. Further down still I saw it where its mile-and-a-quarter of width drops over the Victoria Falls, throwing up that sky-reaching tower of foam which is called 'the smoke that thunders'. I saw all that, the hugeness, the crocodiles, and saw the hippos and learnt with what caution you must treat them; I saw the eagles and the poised knot of vultures that told that there a lion had killed. What, I thought, can be the beginning of such a river - so huge, its further bank so distant - in what deepest heart of Central Africa can it have its beginning? There, there must be the ultimate meaning of the fascination of the sources of rivers. It became obsessional. I must go there; I must find the very first water of this mighty river.

I came to it quite early in the morning when the sun had still not come to its greatest heat. Out of the white blaze of light the ground dropped away down a stony slope into the forest. After the brilliance it was dark until, eyes adjusting, I saw the smooth soaring boles of trees holding the high canopy of their crowns. The sun thrust through its white shafts, finding the clouds of yellow butterflies drifting like sun motes. It was very still, with a silence that is enhanced by occasional sounds. A bird, bell-like, called recurrently: there was a sibilant whisper of insect movement.

Many of the trees stood upon a cluster of aerial roots. In one, secretly inside the roots, there was a small brown pool. It was about twelve inches across. It was the source of the great Zambezi River.

Fulfilment can be found on the banks of the local river. But from childhood, I have felt an urge to explore fishing in all its aspects. It was not until I was over fifty that I first found the great rivers, the jungles, the African wilderness.

But at once there was urgency; flowing from within the roots it went with purpose. And, at once, there was life. Brilliantly metallic beetles skated on the water, lizards slid from my feet and into the water, frogs straddled it.

And there, in this very first water, were fishes, the first fishes, a few inches long, hanging on the infant current. The Zambezi River had begun its life.

If ever I had felt a significance in river sources, here it was verified. In the silence, the soaring tree boles, the intensified shadowed air, there was the sense of being inside a temple. There was a need for hushed voices. There were two with me, and our guide. I had come to make my way from there down all that length of the river that is within Zambia.

We began to walk. Much of the way, I was to walk. And here, not only was there this peculiar magic which river sources have, but here also there was a frontier. The Zambezi's source is in the last most remote north-western extremity of Zambia. Some 50 miles westward lay the frontier with Angola; 50 yards away was the frontier with what was then the Congo but is now Zaire. After that 50 yards the infant Zambezi is the frontier.

This was a time of lawless savagery and upheaval in the Congo: rampant bands of ungoverned Congolese soldiers roamed. I had been warned; they would leave you with nothing but, with luck, your life. Now, walking, we were that tiny river's width inside Zambia; the other bank, a wide step away, was the Congo. Two great countries deeply lost in Central Africa, in this final loneliness.

But it was one forest, one untouched primaeval wilderness threaded through by an eager little river that, already, was pushing its banks apart, becoming deeper. When soon the growth on our Zambian bank became impenetrable and festoons of liana clutched and tripped us, we must cross into the Congo. We made a long stride across the Zambezi River.

Soon that bank too denied us progress; we must cross back into Zambia, and now the river had grown so much that we must jump. We jumped the Zambezi. Now truly it was a small river; one that had chattering rapids - infants that were to become the thundering cataracts of Katima Mulilo. They fell into shadowy pools, five feet and more deep now, with an insistent quiver of life. The first tributary flowed in 30 yards from its source to add its volume. Now we knew we must make the crossing, staggering a passage on fallen tree boles.

The leathery thicket had become so dense as almost to be impassable. But, I thought, the others seem still to be willing; I must struggle on.

The guide stopped; he apologised. He knew I wished to go entirely by the river - but now it was too dense. We must leave the river, go up out of the forest. There we could walk. On the Congo side we climbed out of the corridors of the forest. The ground rose and we passed out of the silent twilight into a drenching blaze of sun. Now at mid-morning the white impact was almost a physical blow.

We walked all day and at evening came to Ikelenge, which was our guide's village. As the short twilight drained he took us to the rest house. The people gathered, the children peered and giggled shyly. Then came the man who had the key of the rest house, and was scolded for keeping us waiting. Then there was a stir; the people fell back.

A man walked into their circle and, reverentially, they all curtsied, softly slapping their hands on thighs, then, as softly, clapping twice. It was the greeting homage for a chief.

The man was big, his manner ceremoniously courteous, his air proud. He was very neat in white shirt and dark blue trousers.

'I am Chief Ikelenge,' he said in good English, 'You must understand I must ask who you are and what is your business.'

I explained, told him that that day we had been at the great river's source.

'And there, at the beginning, did you see the fish?'

Yes, I said, we had seen the fish.

'There is something I must tell you about the fish. You should not try to catch them. However much you cook them they will never die.'

I asked how knowledge of that had come to him.

'It came to me from my forefathers.' As he said it he smiled slightly, inwardly. Chief Ikelenge was smart and modern in his western clothes, and with his dignified amiability; but it was to be seen that he was held in a traditional, almost god-like reverence. Proudly he told me of his people.

'We are of the Ndembu people, who are of the great Lunda tribe. A very long time ago we came here from the Congo, from the Kingdom of Mwantiyanvwa. Still there is the heart of our people.'

Why, I asked, did his people leave there, come out of the Congo to settle here in Zambia?

'That was in the time of the great King Mwantiyanvwa. He was a very great king, great in his pride. He ordered that his people should build so high that he might reach the sky, to bring that within his kingdom. The people built, higher and higher. But the tower was too high; it fell. Many of his people were killed. Now the king was in a very great rage, terrifying his people. They fled, out of the Congo, coming here by the beginning of the great river. Ever since, here the Ndembu people have been.'

As I was to learn, there had been a great migration some 300 years ago: it brought not only the Lunda people, including those of the Ndembu, but also others of the Zambian tribes of today.

Chief Ikelenge, as if now noticing his worshipping subjects, spoke briefly to them for our care; then he left. Until he had gone none dared raise a devout head. Then, talking softly among themselves, they drew together a rough hearth of stones, blew upon its embers. Soon there was a stick fire to which bigger wood was added. The aromatic smoke lay on the air while they, squatting by, put on our cans of baked beans to heat. We, sitting in the dust, drank beer. Who but those who in that climate have walked the day through, can guess the bliss of that beer?

When the children had gone, and soon the men too, the silence of sleep folded over the village. It was probably half-past eight. There was no human sound. We sat on the edge of the rest house veranda, alone in the enormous darkness shrilling with a million insect and other voices. Cicadas kept up their brain-fever singing as they do day and night. The air rustled thickly with insect flight. Insects covered every surface - praying mantises, hornets, monstrous beetles. Over all was the singing of the frogs, filling the night's immensity. Nature's millions were going their private ways: we were irrelevances.

It was my purpose to walk the 50 miles to the Angolan frontier, where I must leave the Zambezi until I rejoined it where it came out of Angola. It was

Fishing is an experience across cultural barriers. But what an incredible range of emotions it stirs from the dark excitement of the Zambezi to the magical mood just after dawn on 16 June at an English tench lake, when no breeze ruffles the water.

97

on this route that I came to Kalene Hill Mission. In Africa there are many missions. Of many of them the less said the better. Kalene Hill Mission was one apart from all others that I saw. It was remote; in Africa's whole continent it could not be more remote, a last niche of Zambia a few miles from Angola and as few from the Congo. As the mission is entered, the hot

ABOVE and RIGHT *I have been drawn to the sources of rivers from the Avon to the Zambezi. And I have been drawn to the sources of fishing in centuries past. What changes in tackle and technique have come about! I drew these two illustrations from my imagination.*

wild bush is left behind; it is spacious, ordered. All is perfectly clean, very self-respecting. Whatever its other purposes, largely it is a hospital.

Kalene Hill was English-run, with some Australians. Its atmosphere was - at my brief visit - one of great serenity. Miss Wentworth conducted us on a tour. She was laconic, matter-of-fact: she was splendid. Whatever may be the effect of missionaries at large, I cannot think it possible that she could bring

anything but good for those in her charge.

She had shown us all, the wards, dispensaries; then she brought us to a building apart.

'Leprosy department,' she said, 'come and see our lepers.'

Some were without hands, some without feet, some with grossly diminished faces. But they were cheerful, apparently happy.

'Can't do anything for their injuries - but we've

stopped the disease. Leprosy doesn't do the damage; it's having no feeling there. They burn themselves, get hurt on things. I think they're pretty happy here.'

To her they were affectionate; and to us very smiling.

'Now. Must show you our witches village.'

She led us away to a place very secluded in the clustering banana and mango trees. Within a screen of matting fencing there was the village, a small replica of those typical of the area - huts made of sun-baked mud bricks, a food store on legs, nothing missing that should be part of a Zambian village. And there the women were, squatting, peeling cassava root (cassava is the basis of the large part of their food). They were scrawny, sagging, wizened, undoubtedly very witchlike.

'They're all witches,' Miss Wentworth said, 'or anyway said to be. Hard to tell really. Cast out of their villages - lucky to get here. If they'd been caught, would have been killed - ritually strangled you know. They're all right now. They'll be here for the rest of their lives. They look terribly old, don't they? Don't suppose they're more than sixty.'

'How are they named as being witches?'

'Oh the witch doctor I expect. Perhaps they failed a test. They appoint a chicken to any woman suspected of being a witch. They give it poison - if it dies the woman is presumed guilty. There was one a while back, found guilty and fled from the village to get here. Never reached us - caught and strangled.

'Now do you see that one, over there? She got here safely; I asked her why she had been accused. She said she ate a person - by that means she ate the spirit of that person; that means she'd die.

'And that one, by the big cassava basket, they said she'd eaten the spirit of her pregnant daughter.

The girl did die. But the woman said she was innocent when we asked her. "Why should I do that to my own daughter?" she said to me. But - on the day the girl died and this woman was accused, the girl's husband took their other child to his own village. Almost at once he and the child died too. You just can't tell.'

Witchcraft and sorcery, Miss Wentworth said, are spread darkly over all aspects of life there, so threaded through every day that it was impossible to be positive as to the innocence or guilt of any of the women. Terror of sorcery is inseparable from all moments of life. It is believed that people become possessed by malevolent spirits of ancestors and other evil spirits: they must be placated constantly. Huts are dedicated to them, set about with all kinds of totems.

It was the day after we had been to Kalene Hill that we came to the Angolan frontier. In the highest heat of afternoon we came to the frontier post. The air was molten, white with heat. In the wooden frontier building it was stifling.

When we had identified ourselves, the men manning the post, courteous and friendly, offered to conduct us down to the actual frontier where the little Jimbe River, a minor feeder of the Zambezi, is to be found. In the fierce clutch of heat we crossed the few hundred yards to the river. We went slowly, moving as sparingly as we could because every slightest movement enhanced the gout of sweat. Then, there it was, the little Jimbe River, perhaps 30 yards wide. But so cravingly, seductively wet. We sat, pressed by the weight of heat, looking at it.

Then one man, as if by compulsion, stood, stripped off his shirt. We said nothing, but all by sudden common purpose, stripped to the minimum of

At one time, quite a large number of species of char, which is a relative of the salmon, were known in British waters. Now only one is known to exist in Britain, Salvelinus alpinus. *It is the same species as the arctic char of the high northern latitudes of Canada and Greenland. The specimen I painted here is one of the Windemere char, which are still caught by local anglers. Char tend to spend a lot of time at great depth but sometimes take flies on the surface. In its breeding colours, the char is a lovely fish to paint, deeply flushed with red on the belly, with white-edged fins and turquoise-green back.*

underwear and plunged in. We swam, came out to dry, swam again.

Now this was at the time of the Angolan war, when Angola's African population, in revolt, was striving against Portugal's army. As we swam, dried and swam, there came along a Portuguese army truck thundering down to the other bank.

It came to a skidding halt; Portuguese soldiers with their automatic weapons threw themselves off. On the bank they threw down their weapons; they stripped off and threw down their uniforms. They too plunged. In mid-river they joined us. So the afternoon went, and we had left it late to return to Ikelenge.

We needed to go back to Ikelenge because from there we must go on by pick-up truck to Mwinilunga, there in the morning to be picked up by air. Our next rendezvous with the Zambezi River must be where it comes out of Angola into Zambia again some hundreds of miles downstream.

The light was thinning when we reached Ikelenge; this was an ominous sign for more than one reason. It was the beginning of the rainy season, a time of very sudden and violent storms. The second reason for worrying was George and the pick-up truck. The truck was not young and had had a hard life; it was battered; it was almost mysteriously unreliable. It would give what appeared to be life's final breath; then George, who was its keeper, would lift the bonnet, hammer with a very large spanner, and the body would stir with new life.

So it had been many times; a time must come, probably soon, with no return to life. This had to be our link to Mwinilunga over rough bush tracks and three rivers to cross. Already there were signs; the sky was lowering; faint blue flickers of light animated it.

So, what of George? He had been lent to us by the District Secretary in Mwinilunga, he and the truck. George was young with a black face that seemed to beam with such white-toothed innocence. But, as we found, he was not quite like that. He was homicidal, seeking to run down women on the road bearing their cassava root bundles. Driving the truck he knew only one speed, the truck's maximum, about 55 mph.

Now, in Ikelenge, the truck was in one of its catalepsies: George was noisily within its bonnet. The air was changing. Thin whiffles of wind came stirring the stillness, rustling the leaves, brushing chill on our faces. The short twilight passed; night fell purple-black, a close shroud. Now lightning was showing distantly. It grew quickly, it and the thunder leaping the miles until a shivering blue brilliance put a ghostly light on everything. Thunder towered and rolled in mountains of sound that seemed to press in our skulls. Now the wind rose to huge gusts like giant hands pushing us. As yet the rain had not come. It would come, devastatingly.

When it comes it can completely wash away the infirm substance of bush roads. And those three rivers - only small in the dry season, little more than dongas, sometimes even dry - but the rainy season storms turn them to furiously raging torrents. There were bridges over them, just crosswise logs with no guard rails. Half-an-hour's delay might be the last half-hour of possible passage.

We waited. George had no sense of uneasiness. Idly, he fiddled under the bonnet.

Then, rattling, blowing and snoring, life returned to the truck. Would it survive as far as Mwinilunga; would it live through what we knew to be coming? Could it do that in George's hands?

We started; then so did the rain. At first the enormous drops fell separately, then increased, came together, became a solidity of water dropped in continuous mass. The storm rose to bursting frenzy. Lightning tore the night with eerie lucidities of light punctuated at first by intervals of total blackness. Then there were no intervals; the whole world crouched under an unbroken blue-white shiver. Blinding plunges of lightning to earth filled the night's circumference.

Even George, it could have been thought, should have been awed into care. He threw the truck at the night, smiling his white-toothed smile.

We shouted, we ordered. We beseeched that he should drive more slowly. He went on just as wildly as we slewed on the disintegrating road.

'George,' we bellowed at him, 'there'll be floods. Drive more slowly!' We slid on the road with lessening sense of contact. Sliding violently round a bend, we found the road had become a lake. For a moment even the thunder's roar was submerged by our impact. The wall of displaced water dropped on us like stone. George did not lift his foot; we bucketed on, thrashing without vision behind the wall of water of our making.

As if by a miracle, we emerged. 'George,' we shouted, 'slow down - you'll flood the engine.' But George was smiling.

The hardship of fishing in a downpour is often offset by the increased prospect of catching a fish, as the air pressure changes and the water is freshened and re-oxygenated. But never again have I experienced rain like I did in Zambia...

The road was breaking up quickly, the dagger-thrust of rain prizing away such small foundation as it had. Now floods on the road became more frequent. George kept his foot down, assaulting the floods as if to kill them. The windscreen wipers stopped. George bashed the brakes. In the cold blue fire of lightning we lay in the water. George, out and under the bonnet, used his spanner punishingly. When he climbed back the wipers worked.

On we went until in the midst of the next flood the engine stopped. Then we knew; he had done it. He had flooded the engine.

But George smiled. He wrought with his spanner. He came back and the engine started. Only the devil as partner could bring quite such sinister providence.

Now little of the road was entirely above water: there was no secure hold for the truck. We slewed sickeningly, each tree an approaching crisis. Then the road dipped from under us.

It was dropping to the first river; its surface was gone; it was nothing but sludge. We could see the river's roaring torrent. George, seized by panic snatched on the brakes.

We slid, we accelerated, this way, that way: George clutched the disassociated wheel. We were lurching headlong off the road, askew to the river. With disaster's clarity I saw the bridge's narrow span as we slewed away from it. We were jammed in the cab with no chance for movement.

Now here was the water. In the fury of impact, in the drench of spray we shuddered and were into another skid. Sidelong and diagonally we were up from the water, over the shoulder, half sideways onto the rail-less bridge. We crossed, skidding, feeling the wheels slide over the edge, this side then that side. We came off sideways, zig-zagged up the slope, straightened, stopped. We had, it must be supposed, hit a rock by the water, starting the skid which saved us. George's devil was with him. He at last was sobered. He drove us now with comparative care; our crossing of the other two rivers was done with no more than the inescapable danger.

With that last bridge crossed, almost in a minute - such is the strange way of tropical storms - the fury fell from the storm. The lightning died, the rain stopped. Nature seemed to sigh, then smile. The peace seemed to be as heaven is imagined. The next morning the world was wonderful, cleared and clean after the storm.

Of what else happened as I made my way down the Zambezi there is no room to tell here; anyway, I did write a book about it, *Coming Down The Zambezi* (Constable, 1974).

Of my final peaceful reaching of Zambia's last inches by the Zambezi River I tell elsewhere in this book. But I must mention the man with a rifle. This was at the time when Zambia and what then was Rhodesia were in a state of armed confrontation. Rhodesia was just across the river; this was the Front Line. Not long since, a Landrover had been blown up by a land mine on a local road. Nevertheless a spirit of great peace lay in the air - or so it appeared to me, and in the afternoon, my journey done, I walked back a few miles into Zambia, past scattered villages, where blue mountains stopped the distance and the track was pink with the dust of old volcanic rock.

In the evening to the rest house there came this man. He was big of belly and he wore nothing but a pair of khaki shorts: and he carried a ·303 rifle.

The Dunn, a tributary of the Kennet, seen here at Freeman's Marsh near Hungerford. As on many of the chalkstreams nowadays, rainbow and brown trout are stocked, but a residue of wild brownies still manage to co-exist.

He announced himself as Zambia's Chief of Police, answerable only to the President. Conversationally I said something of my afternoon walk.

'If I had seen you,' he said, 'I would have shot you first and asked questions afterwards.'

Though I think his stated credentials were unlikely, I think it not unlikely that he would have shot me.

So mundane is the modern world that even in Africa's remoteness such passing incidents have to serve you to make a sense of adventure. The world has shrunk, is too much known for the sense of adventure in the old frame. In my boyhood - a long time ago - we gorged on the adventure stories of such as Henty and Ballantyne. In the same frame, for adults as well as boys, there was *Moby Dick*, the truest kind of adventure story, and very much of a kind that could not outlast the nineteenth century. The raw cruel deadliness of such adventure could hardly be envisaged in the cosseted enclosure of the twentieth century. So I would have sworn.

But I was told of the Azores. In the Azores men were still going out in small open boats, with hand harpoons and hand lances, to hunt the great sperm whales; still pitting themselves against the perilous ocean. The twentieth century had produced the obscene efficiency of the factory whaleship and the modern harpoon gun. Why then should there still be men day by day facing such appalling perils? It seemed not of our time, not of this century.

And the Azores? What did I know of the Azores? A remote mid-ocean group of islands associated with weather forecasts. How great their isolation must be. The thought could set a frightened tingle in the imagination.

Max Reinhardt had recently published my book, *The Gentle Art of Angling,* and it was he who told me this wild story. Would I go, he asked? Would I go with these hardly-credible whalers, go with them to sea, share their wild vocation, and then write a book about it?

There was not even a direct way to get there. For part of the way I could go in contemporary fashion - from Lisbon in a modern aeroplane down to Madeira, then up to Santa Maria which is the most easterly of the islands. From there today's world began to fall away. Still I could travel on by air, but now by the little DC3, that which during the last war was known as the Dakota - small, unpressurised, looking antediluvian. Dawdling at low altitude it took me to Terceira; there, it and the world of today left me. There I had to wait till a little ship should take me on through the islands to one called Fayal. There, and at its sister island, Pico, the other side of a five-mile strait, the nineteenth century lived on.

In all the world there could be few pleasanter places for waiting than Terceira. The only reason the world acknowledges it at all is because on that oceanic speck there is a United States air base. Thus it has a runway; thus I, coming out of the twentieth century, could get there.

But beyond; beyond there was no such convenience. I must wait till Friday when a little ship would enter the harbour. And on that following Friday, in the sparkling light of dawn, there it was, *Espirito Sancto*, tied up and ready to take us aboard. 'Us' was a mixed cargo: people returning to their islands, a large old-fashioned mangle, a cow and a mule, and all sorts of boxes and bundles. I went on the minute upper deck against the small stump of funnel, sharing it with black-shawled old peasant women, a young soldier going to his leave, men under wide flat straw hats. Now the ship was crammed to its small capacity, the siren sounded and we left the last remnant of the contemporary world.

As soon as the sea took us, those island folk aboard became ill: the high sounds of distress were on every side. But the sea air was good; care could be taken to be as much upwind as possible.

That voyage-in-a-day was interminable, being not just one of miles traversed, but more of a progress of decline out of the twentieth century and into the nineteenth. We went westerly from island to island, calling here, that the cow might be belly-sling landed on a slip notched into the sheer of a precipice, there that the mule might similarly go ashore. At another

place a little black-garbed old woman had a boat lowered so that she and her mangle could be put ashore. The voyage, timeless, more dream than real, took us till the evening. Then leaving Pico under its volcanic peak we crossed that last strait. There, for me, was the last island. There was the little town of Horta on this island of Fayal, pastel-painted against the sea dark with evening.

I expect that the Fayal I knew has gone. The twentieth century has jumped the islands now, putting down airstrips on all of them. I found Fayal as the nineteenth century of New England had left it. That was the time of Moby Dick, when the whale-ships went out of the ports of Nantucket and New Bedford to hunt the great sperm whale. So going in mid-ocean they found the Azores, islands thrown up by volcanic eruption.

They are green and quiet now, peaceful and immensely fertile. But, beneath, the old fiery rumble is still there. Only a few years before I was there, a new volcano had thrown up a cone from the sea, joining it to Fayal, and there had been an earthquake which had left an open trench across the high top of the island. As the islands are, so are the men - gentle peaceful men who in a moment can erupt, and they have a matching intrepidness. The New England whalers found them apt material for the searingly perilous business of whaling. Many Azoreans joined the Yankee ships.

The passing of the nineteenth century saw the decline and end of New England whaling: the old fearsome trade was over. So it seemed. In the Azores - not in the New World, not in the Old - things went on as before. Open-boat whaling had been learnt from the New Englanders. The Azoreans adapted it to their own circumstances, launching whale boats from the shore, not from ships. The islands were the ships. The New England boats, called canoas (pronounced *canooa*) were 27 feet long; those of the Azores 37 feet - boats as long as that, if lowered from ships, would break their backs. They are light, canoe-shaped, pointed at both ends, designed for agile manoeuvrability: for that they sacrifice much of their sea-worthiness. They are boats for easy seas: if caught in heavy weather, as sometimes has happened, they cannot survive for long.

The crew is seven men. In the bows is the harpooner, who also pulls an oar. Astern from him are five men pulling oars alternate sides. In the stern is the boatheader. He commands the boat, uses the rudder when the boat is under sail, or the 22 foot steering oar when going with oars.

In the point of the bows, at the top of the stem, there is a cleft; this is the chock, for the running of the whale line when a whale is fastened. Within the swell of the bows there is a sunken, decked-in area called the box. It is for holding the coiled box-warp, those few fathoms of lighter line between the harpoon and the whale line.

At the after edge of the box, crossing from gunwale to gunwale, is the clumsy cleat or thigh-board. It is a heavy plank which has in it, a little left of centre, a semi-circular notch. In this the harpooner braces his left thigh when using the harpoon or lance.

On the starboard side, leaning against the clumsy cleat are the harpoons and lances. In the stern the last few feet are decked in; this is the cuddy board. On the cuddy board stands the loggerhead, a bollard about eight inches high, tapered outwards from base to top. That is the crucial tool in the playing of a whale. Line is stored in two tubs amidships. It comes from the tub astern to the loggerhead, round the loggerhead, then up the centre line of the boat to where it joins the box warp which is coiled in the box. Each tub holds 120 fathoms of line.

That - this frail boat, the simple tools and weapons - is the whole means by which the mighty sperm whale is hunted. A bull sperm whale may occasionally reach 65 feet long. It may therefore be seen that open-boat whaling is very dangerous indeed, and first-hand experience of it does not lessen that impression. I, sitting in Café Sport in Horta, much frequented by people of the sea, and past and present whalers, heard the stories.

There was the tale told of that young man who gave promise to become a fine harpooner. On his first day of real hunting, when he had successfully fastened his whale, the leaping line took him by the ankle: he was never seen again. On another day, a whale had been harpooned, then lanced. In its enormous anguish it turned on the canoa, chopped it along its length to matchwood. And so on, the tragedies of many whaling days.

Before I could go to sea with the whalers, there was one compulsory act: I must call upon the Captain of the Port to sign a document. This paper is known, colloquially, as the Death Warrant. It is a declaration that if death or accident should come to

me while at sea with the whalers the responsibility is my own alone, exonerating all others.

My first season was one of bad weather. Day by day the skies were mostly dark and the wind strenuous. Good whaling weather is sunny, calm, with the wind mainly from the north. In such conditions the binocular lookouts, at stations of overlapping cones of vision all round the island, can see a 'blow' quite far out to sea, 30 and more miles. But, that first season, every morning as first light filtered over the harbour, I found shaking heads among those who crewed the tow launches. 'No

ABOVE *No fish has so many variations as the brown trout,* Salmo trutta. *So diverse are they that they used to be considered different species altogether. But* Salmo trutta *they are, including the seatrout. The model for this picture was one of those large, plump specimens from the River Test at Leckford. After I had made my study the fish was returned to the water.*

baleia today,' they said. *Baleia* is the Portuguese word for whale - and in the Azores it is a word for igniting action. But now, each day, there was no action.

Then, one morning in the Café Sport, when time had slipped to 11 o'clock with desultory minutes falling away, there was the hissing rise, the thunderous burst - the rocket! The rocket's signal - a blow had been sighted.

Now I was running to the tow launches - I and all those whalers, out of Café Sport, out of doors,

pouring out from the little street under Burnt Mountain, all shouting, 'Baleia! Baleia!' Now we were in the tow launches, churning white wakes out of the harbour and racing under the snarling heights until we came to Salao. The canoes were waiting, just off the slip, pitching on the ragged swell, looking frail. Their crews had a fiercely wild look, as the whalers invariably had: dark, sea-bitten under their wide rush hats. Piratical men.

Now we had taken their tows; engines roared,

When I was commissioned to paint four watercolours for framed prints (of which this is one) it was my aim to give each picture the essential feeling of the type of fishing involved. This is of pike fishing and I wanted to convey the kind of soft day in winter in which the light is low and the pike are surging at the small fry.

wakes streamed, land dropped astern. Now fear had drained but left its raw-edged energy. The cold in the belly was still tautly there; eyes were hard, jaws tight. The radio barked, directing course, checking, that in all that lopping waste of sea we should find the whale that was, somewhere, 'having its spoutings out'. Among those men with me, in so much sea, there seemed to be a certainty that this blow, once raised, would not be lost.

Suddenly we had stopped. We lay in a void of sea, as it seemed to me, out of time, out of other worlds. But to the men there was shape, there was a sense of proximity.

A canoa was hauled up on its warp, bringing its bows alongside. From the stern the stroke oar clambered forward and aboard the launch. I, dropping into the canoa, teetered down the cramped and bouncing boat to the stern. I found inches of space at the feet of the boatheader. His bare feet, horny-thick below his rolled, patched and baggy pantaloons, were on the standing cleats either side. His air was swingeing. High on the cleats he had a piratical majesty under the wide brim and high crown of his straw hat.

'The tub oar, my neighbour forward in the boat, was elderly, lean, big-boned, brown and textured like a nut. He too wore the high-crowned straw hat; the eyes that looked out from under it, half smiling, a little shy, were gentle and experienced, eyes that had seen much life. His eyes were blue and, as detail will impinge in such scarifying moments, I saw that they were faded round the edges, as if much sea-searching had drawn the colour from them.' So I said in the book I wrote about my whaling adventures, *Baleia! Baleia! The Whalers of the Azores.*

I quote again - then memory was sharp, still with its edge undimmed:

'I thought now was the moment, now we would cast off our tow, now the men would bend to the great oars, the hunt would begin. But *Walkiria*, the tow launch, burst to noisy life again, the warp snapped taut. We were in tow with the boatheader on his standing cleats scanning ahead, commanding *Walkiria* with shout and sweep of arm.

A ferocious splendour had come upon him, a seeming of enlargement, a combustion. Bear to starboard, his wide thrust of arm commanded. He roared and imprecated at *Walkiria* as she strove to his directing. The high angry flood of words poured from him; he flung a sinewed spread of fingers at the sky, shook his head like the rolling of a planet. The cindery gout of his words scorched across at *Walkiria* while his eyes searched ahead. So we went, searching, veering, bouncing in *Walkiria's* wake.

'The hoarse roar of the boatheader continued, bludgeoning *Walkiria* to his bidding. Then I saw his eyes fasten, seeming to contract. In the midst of his thunder he dropped his eyes to mine, with barely perceptible nod and smile, a brief friendly private signal. He had raised the whale. His voice rose to crescendo, his arm's sweep ordered the casting of the tow. Suddenly then he relaxed, softened; he turned to me, rolled his head widely. "Eeeee - Caramba!" he said.

'*Walkiria* veered away, distance soon soaked up the sound of her. We lay rolling in the immensity of quiet. There was a change in the boat. There had been engine's roar and churn of water, tension's release in angry shouting. Now there was this envelopment of quiet, the soft sound of water, the

transfiguration of the boatheader. There was none but he and his crew now; he spoke softly, nearly whispering, directing the intense almost silent activity, directing like a gentle father. Soundless excitement wrapped the boat, a sort of elation.

'The harpooner had come aft to midships, bending the line from the waist tub to that of the after tub and that to the box line of the harpoon. His movements were tight, nerve-strung, his face hard-set, but his actions precise and certain. He was a young man, lean and wiry as a thorn bough. Then he was ready with first and second irons to his right against the thigh board; all was ready, the long oars out, the boatheader on his cleats with the great steering oar. The men bent to the stroke, a long easy powerful stroke. They were smiling.

'They rowed, and I had no consciousness of direction in all that roll of sea; the boatheader was above me laying his weight to the steering oar, eyes scanning the dark heave. We were alone, no boat near; recurrently I saw one other of the canoes showing for moments, and there, distant, showing no

more than mast and wheelhouse, was a launch, and I was not able to know if she was *Walkiria* of Cetaceo.

'Then the boatheader looked at me, nodded, pointed with his head beyond our bows. He spoke quietly to the crew, one word: "Forca" he said.

'Still to my searching eyes, low in the boat, there was nothing, nothing but the immense horizon-rimmed green heave of sea. But I knew, all knew that he, upraised there, had seen the whale, had seen it sounding out. Fear was gone now, leaving only strung elation. The men quickened stroke, smiling, smiling. Only the harpooner did not smile. His face was rigid, stone-set.'

There was to be no whale that day. That one that sounded was not seen again - it was the fairly exceptional one, a lost whale. Exceptional because the whaler's sense of where a sounded whale will re-emerge for its blows is uncanny. So we lay, the hunt over, until *Walkiria* came up to take our tow. The sky was darkening; in the churn of *Walkiria*'s wake we turned towards Fayal lying under the horizon. The world was empty but for *Walkiria* and us.

Then it was not. The porpoises came, out of the loneliness, a crowd of slipping satiny creatures, hooping in the swell. They showed first 50 yards off, but closed in till they were a hand's touch away. They were all about, a merry escort, innocently companionable. One attached itself to me; I felt its conscious companionship. As each parabola cleared it from the sea its turning eye sought mine, it and all of them coming as intimately close as sea and boat allowed. So they came with us, through the miles until in the declining light the black shape of Fayal rose from under the horizon. They would come no nearer man's land; with a sense of farewell they left us. The rocket sounded no more for me that season. Until the next season I returned to the twentieth century, until the nineteenth should call me back. In July that came. I was back in Horta after that same timeless voyage in a day through the islands.

At first there were days that, though fine and full of sun, were not whaling days. The wind was out of the south and rough, not giving the calm sea and far visibility which is good for whaling. But there came an evening when they said, 'Tomorrow will be good; the wind is going round to north. The sea will be calm, the lookouts will be able to see the blows.' And, so, as the stars faded, as the darkness thinned at 4am I was on the way to Castelo Branco, because there in a precarious notch in the crags is a tiny harbour where lie the whaleboats. There, when I came, they were waiting - José Fula, Antonio, and those others, all of them Fula brothers, who man the canoas. Expectation was hard in the air.

But time built slowly. First light rose glinting on the sea in that queer interval between dawn and sunrise. Moments ticked off separately because each one could be that one when the knell should sound. At 6.40am there was the hissing gush of sound. It hung: then the rocket's explosion. Far to sea the blow had been seen. As the sun's first blinding lances

dazzled, we were running down the slip. We threaded out past the dead lava fangs, tows were taken. We went westward under the fierce sheer of coast, and now the sun was climbing, moltenly blazing over the stern. The sky had not one least wisp of cloud. It was the perfection of whaling weather.

We passed Capelinhos on our beam, and as it fell astern we veered north of west. Fayal was over the stern and Pico translucent on the port quarter. Then, two hours out, Fayal was low under the stern and softening. When the fourth hour had nearly gone men went to the mast heads to scan the glitter of the sea's recession, to me as enigmatic as through the hours before. But in the boats now there was taut expectancy. The launches stopped, tows cast. The boats were separating. *S. Jaoa Baptista*, José Fula's canoa, with sails hoist and taking the wind, bore away to starboard with certainty as if running on a beam, scudding up the sea distances.

Then there was the blow, a stubby mushroom, mushroom pinkish-brown. On *S. Jaoa Baptista* the paddles were out, the men sitting on the gunwales facing forward, digging with swift rhythm so that the boat seemed to skim. The moments shivered, Antonio, who was harpooner, was at the clumsy cleat, thigh in the thigh notch, braced like a stretched wire. And there was the blow again, close now. José in the stern took the boat round so that it should come directly at the great sheer of the whale's head - going *cabeca con cabeca* - head on head, that most perilous of all approaches, coming within that narrow cone of no vision between the whale's eyes.

At the last second he flicked the boat round the head into vision, then passed - the second of most searing danger. Antonio exploded from his feet, the harpoon was 'darted'. The whale was 'fastened'. In the huge smother of sea the whale's great flukes had gone up, a deadly menace hung momentarily over the boat. Now there was the hissing of running line, tumbling away through the chocks and the boat tossing on the maelstrom.

The whale ran deeply, the line throbbing and jumping after, and the man at the tub oar ladling water on it smoking at the loggerhead. Then the whale stopped. The line was rising. The sea burst; there was the whale, enormous and grey, thrashing in the white toss of sea, blowing and blowing. José had taken a turn at the loggerhead but could not keep it. The mighty flukes threw up, the monstrous back rounded out. The whale had sounded. The line was pouring away.

Its runs were shorter, not as deep. Then it was lifting, then again the eruptive burst of sea. It blew, thrashing, running in the surface with boiling wake. José took turns at the loggerhead, held them; the bows plunged, took water. The canoa was towing, scudding along in the whale's wake at fifteen knots or more. This was the 'Nantucket Sleigh Ride'. Again I quote from that written when memory was sharp:

'So we went for a quarter of a mile till the flukes peaked again and the whale sounded and José must let go his hold at the loggerhead. The great pestered striving creature was tiring though; in only minutes it surfaced, beating and rolling, and now I caught the sound of its blow, windy with distance, a softened gravelly sigh of sound.

'The men were up, astride the thwarts; they were hauling, creeping slowly on the whale. Now it lifted its flukes, slapped them down, lifted them again seeking to sound, but now with the beginning of an impotence. In its confusion and anger it lifted its huge bluff of head, rolled it, then was running again, snatching away the hauled line, towing the boat. It was staccato, in a huge tormented bother, running, stopping, with intermittent lifting of ineffectual flukes. The men hauled, gave line, creeping nearer, coming with their brave midget impertinence upon the now spent but frantic quarry.

'It was running no more; it lunged and rolled and beat at the surface. Now I could see its length, a grey enormity of a creature, 60 feet long at a guess, an angry and desperate giant, so direfully beset by a shadowy enemy outside its conception. It was making a lurching ambit about the boat now, a slow shaking circling, 150 yards off, blowing and thrashing and tired, but too hugely threatening still for nearer approach. It seemed to have fallen into a blind

This oil is entirely imaginery, but it arises from the powerful image that the pike conjures up. We never know with certainty just how awesomely huge the fish may be, lurking in its obscure watery haunts.

tormented anger, lifting and shaking its head, throwing up and dropping helpless flukes.

'S. *Jaoa Baptista* meanwhile stood by, waiting, wary of this still too menacing monster, taking line when it slackened but keeping safety's optimum distance. In the bows Antonio stood, arms hanging, patient for the moment of decision. Now the whale had paused in its boiling circuit, lying in one place, beating still with flippers and flukes, but resting a little from its worst fury.

'The oars were put out; Antonio, bracing and stiffening in the bows, picked up the lance. The boat moved forward slowly, stroke by stroke, creeping on the whale. A renewed convulsion of fury came upon it, the boat paused, blades out till the moment passed and the whale lay in a suspension of fatigue. Now the oars were in, stroking quickly, going fast on the quarry before opportunity should pass, Antonio braced in a forwardly-angled poise against the thrust of right leg.

'The seconds went down like audible ticks, each at painful length, with the whale stirring and yawing and Antonio with the lance in rigid readiness above his head. At almost the last second's drop the whale humped, churned flukes and flippers. But the canoa, too close for hesitation, went in. At two fathom's distance, obliquely on the flipper, Antonio detonated, making his plunging tossing throw. The lance was in, the whale in awful frenzy lunging away while the boat tittupped crazily on the smother. As the men backed water two strokes, Antonio doubled, throwing back his weight to draw out the lance.

'So it continued. At each more frequent opportunity the canoa went in, Antonio plunging the lance, the whale's bouts of movement weakening.

Once the whale, deadly stricken now, sought to sound, throwing up the awful canopy of its flukes over the canoa. The boat, backing water, escaped their down smash. But a time came: Antonio had lanced once more: the grey immensity of wounded body lashed and shuddered; it blew with a thickened sighing gush of sound. The blow was red, no longer atomised, thickly bloody, an awful bloody gush.

'The whale was truly in its preposterous decline. Though it fought still, still made vast convulsive movements, the more quiescent punctuations came oftener. Now it was blowing recurrently, a repeating gush, and the blue had gone from the sea. Men and monster fought in a widening heave of blood. How, I wondered, could even this great creature persist so pitifully in its remnant of life?

'A change came upon it; its beating died away. It had begun to go in a slow weaving perambulation. Then, slowly, it sank a little; so it was for moments. Then, abruptly, explosively, its head burst from the sea vertically, a full ten feet. It hung there for moments, the huge parallel of head; it opened its mouth to a gape, clashed its jaws. Then it collapsed into the sea.

'Now the boats backed away, stood off; here was 'the flurry'. With S. *Jaoa Baptista* at its axis, the whale moved in a wide circle, labouring spasmodically. Once it lifted from the water, half its depth, with a convulsion running through it, then fell back in a beat of surge. Once it lifted its flukes, slapped them down explosively. Perhaps its life went from it then, perhaps it flickered on for a time. It still dragged its heavy course for a little longer, then lay motionless in the lift of swell, with one flipper standing rigidly. It was dead, 'fin out'.

'A strange peace had come: all seemed spent, all time, all action. The drama was done. We lay in the long swell, blue again, the four boats and the launches in a cluster in the oceanic emptiness, and in the midst of us the grey, lifeless undulation of the whale.

'Then, like men stirring from a dream, the crew of *S. Jaoa Baptista* hauled up slowly on the line, coming with another of the canoas to reeve the towing strap at the tail of the prize. It was all done so slowly, as with a sort of lethargy of contentment of freedom from danger and from striving. We, the rest of us, slumped where we were, loosely abandoned to the sea's roll.'

So ended the primaeval encounter. Such a thing of the nineteenth century as that was, was as far removed from our time as the hunting of the mammoth. It belonged to a time when man was one animal among others, subject to jungle law. Theirs was a contest for subsistence in which one side or the other would survive. So great was the danger of each day of Azorean whaling that at each evening's reunion the men's families met them with clinging relief and gratitude for one more return.

It is all done now: Azoreans go no more to their dire assignments. For that I am glad. I never knew for whom I was more painfully sorry - the poor giant pestered into death, or those men, pitifully poor, of giant bravery who, so often, came to disaster. They were centuries away from the safe butchers in the modern factory ships.

My watercolour shows the lovely spate river Erriff flowing under the mountains of County Mayo, Ireland.

CHAPTER EIGHT

Art

I am an artist; I am a painter and a sculptor; I am a loving practitioner in the sweet art of drawing. With much fulfilment I have worked as a designer and a typographer. I cannot imagine not being these things. Saying so might suggest that such as I are oddities, throw-offs from normality. Most certainly that is not so: to be an artist - one of any consequence anyway - is to be a special expression of the normal, a distilling of what is felt, in varying degree, by a majority of people, given the chance. Most people given that chance, can at least sometimes find delight in having life in a beautiful world. The artist in his work has the gift of isolating and enshrining those pleasures so that they are the more keenly experienced by others.

That which makes me an artist, makes it impossible for me not also to be an angler. The instinctive sources of both are very close. He who is exultant in the air of an early summer morning, who is enchanted by the smell of rivers in sinking summer evenings, is fascinated by the shadowed obscurities of weir pools and glides under hollowed river banks, is undoubtedly on his way to being an angler. If he has the necessary ability he cannot fail to be drawn by these things into expression as an artist. In the whole aspect of nature there is an irresistible stimulus to an artist's activity; and in water that is intensified. To take from an eddy greenly shadowed under the bank a big blunt-headed chub, could almost turn a stone to painting. There is this chavender, thick-shouldered, with its large sculptured head, brassy-scaled, coral-finned, lacquered and shining. Could there be anything more beautiful, more wonderful to emerge from the water?

To say such things at this point in history might be misunderstood. I speak of being an artist, of painting and sculpting; I am speaking of what that has meant down the centuries until this century. Through that time as far back as human record, the artist's central stimulus has been worship of having life in a lovely world (sometimes that has been overlaid by religious themes, but that has been because the church was the main patron; then as at other times, the artist has needed an employer).

Our deplorable species has destroyed much of what was so worshipful on our planet as nature gave it to us: but in spite of man's appalling treatment of nature, that which we still have is stimulus enough to make men anglers and stir artists to creation.

But the word is artist - it no longer presents a clearly understandable image. When a man piles tyres together, calls it sculpture, is applauded, and richly paid; what then does 'artist' mean?

At the Royal Academy a few years ago there was an exhibition of the works of Sir Joshua Reynolds. It was a splendid show in spite of some pictures having suffered colour loss and loss from the work of the master's assistants. We emerged from the last room uplifted. In the adjoining room there was a very large modern canvas, honoured with a place of great prominence. I thought it bad beyond description; ugly, without any trace at all of the skills and vision of painting. It seemed a dishonour to the building in which it was hung.

In the Royal Academy's Summer Exhibition it is the practice annually to award a prize for the work judged to be the 'most distinguished' in the show. I have seen very few of them: those I have seen have been inept, clumsy, lacking skills of composition, drawing, and painting techniques.

The more superior newspapers support art critics who keep us briefed as to the climate of the 'World of Art'. Of those I have read, what they write has been spurious poppycock, meaning nothing. It is incomprehensible that these vapourings can be taken seriously; the nonsense is so obvious. Portentous webs of words are spun which have nothing even remotely to do with the simple glorious urge which impels an artist - a real artist.

In all history there has been no other time when art has been so degraded. Many people indoctrinated by the critics, learn a jargon; they affect admiration for what quite plainly is not art at all, and which they cannot, sincerely, admire.

It should not be thought that the real artist has become extinct. Unseen by this fashionable world, he continues. His time might even come again. May it be so.

I am a sculptor; in former times so to describe myself would have defined me. Now it does not. It could mean that I group rubbish in piles; it could mean that I weld old bicycles into bundles, or that I pile building bricks, put on the top an empty soup can and in that a lavatory brush. It would be exhibited and there surrounded by earnest people studying it, seeking to find its profound message.

But I am a sculptor; I do not do those things. I

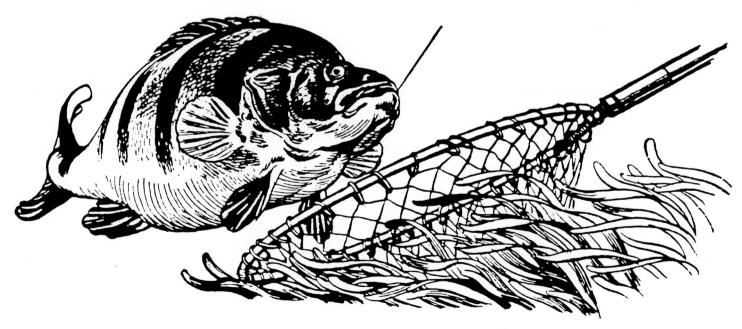

see a log of wood or a piece of stone. In my mind there is a conception of something of beauty and of meaning hidden within that wood or stone. I, being a sculptor, can carve away what is outside to reveal what is within. That is what sculpture means. That is what it must have meant to Michelangelo. The story of the Emperor's new clothes remains a basic statement of truth about people and credulity.

I am a sculptor but, unhappily, am able to do only very little of it. The carving of wood and stone is extremely demanding of time, and artists have as much need as other people to earn a living. Because of that, and because all the other

LEFT *An illustration from* The Angler's Companion *of a perch being drawn to the net. The barred flanks, red fins and spiny dorsals make this one of the most exciting fish for the young angler to catch.*

RIGHT *Self portrait in pencil.*

LEFT *I have found great happiness in the creation of books, none more so than* The Angler's Companion, *published in 1958. I had the great pleasure of producing the book single-handedly, and had a wonderful time. This is the dust jacket I designed for the first edition.*

ABOVE *I carved this Shire horse from a log of pearwood, a particularly lovely wood for carving: even-grained and with the perfect texture for polishing with beeswax. There can be few better subjects for the sculptor than this noble horse.*

ABOVE *Here is another imaginary scene, one that is clearly implanted in my mind's eye. It is that time of summer when the trout season is moving on and there will be no hatch until the light begins to fade. But on this sunny morning, a trout does rise - it may well be of the once-only kind, and therefore should be covered at once.*

forms of creative art are also extremely demanding of my time, sculpture cannot have all the devotion it deserves.

As an art student, and later as an artist and writer I have always worked very hard. Now, at the age of 86, I am still working hard. I am happy so to do, and day by day I am conscious of how much still there is to do. To have life in a beautiful world, to be so doubly blessed as to be both a fisherman and an artist - nearly related things - is to me a great happiness.

Working as an artist I have wandered widely; on the whole, the wandering has been fun. Sometimes the fun has had dilutents. In 1933 the great Advertising Exhibition was held at Olympia - the only one, I believe, that there has been.

One exhibitor at the show was the advertising agency Mather & Crowther; their most important account was the 'Eat More Fruit' campaign. They used it as the theme for their stand. The stand was triangular, and for each of its sides there was to be a mural over the whole area illustrating the Eat More Fruit theme. I was commissioned to design and paint the murals. To do that I had three weeks, a very tightly minimal time. By losing no minute I

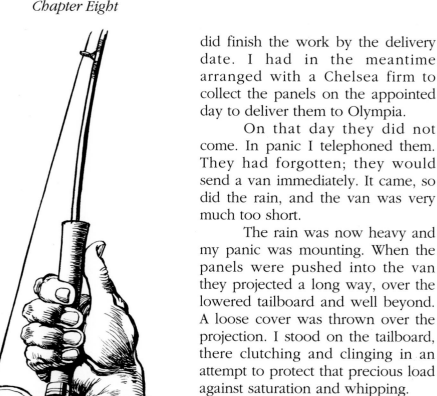

did finish the work by the delivery date. I had in the meantime arranged with a Chelsea firm to collect the panels on the appointed day to deliver them to Olympia.

On that day they did not come. In panic I telephoned them. They had forgotten; they would send a van immediately. It came, so did the rain, and the van was very much too short.

The rain was now heavy and my panic was mounting. When the panels were pushed into the van they projected a long way, over the lowered tailboard and well beyond. A loose cover was thrown over the projection. I stood on the tailboard, there clutching and clinging in an attempt to protect that precious load against saturation and whipping.

Thus, from Croydon up to

Left *I have always believed that clear technical drawings like this are the best medium for conveying practical angling information. Perhaps this is one of the reasons why Mr Crabtree was so effective in teaching many young anglers in the 1950s to fish.*

RIGHT *The River Usk, a favourite fishing haunt of mine and of my late friend Terry Thomas.*

Olympia the journey was made, arriving without disaster. But at Olympia the delivery yard was flooded. Nevertheless, with wading and splashing, the panels were got inside. They were taken to the stand and I stood in attendance to see them safely set in their designated places. At last all was done. Clutching the remnants of my nervous system I took myself to the bar for what was urgently needed. I was very quickly joined by a deeply agitated Managing Director of Mather & Crowther.

'The bloody fool,' he gasped.

'Can you come? The bloody fool - he's cut the hole in the wrong place.'

I went; there was the 'bloody fool' standing in

uneasy 19-year-old nonchalance. His job had been to cut a hole in a prescribed place for a projector. He had cut the hole, but he had cut it in the middle of one of my panels, obliterating a pile of oranges. How it was that the materials for repair were there I cannot remember. Perhaps in caution I had brought them. I made the repair and returned to the bar for the seriously needed restorative.

During the second Great War I did many things for the Ministry of Information. I designed the decoration of exhibition stands: I did a strip cartoon biography of Winston Churchill. For a time at Ealing Studios I worked on cartoon films for the Ministry of Food. I also spent much time squeezed into the

ABOVE *The flounder is not generally regarded as a freshwater species but it does often migrate from the sea long distances up rivers. In fact, they will often go as far as they can, until stopped by an obstruction such as a weir. There was a time when they ascended the Severn as far inland as Shrewsbury. But that was before the weirs were built. I painted this flounder from a living specimen at the saltwater research laboratory at Lowestoft.*

LEFT *This picture is called 'To the Coven' meaning 'to the witches coven or gathering'. This is not an actual place, but one symbolically imagined. It is an allegorical painting, a genre in which I have become increasingly fascinated. The figures are what I perceive as architypally rural.*

bellies of tanks so that I could produce drawings of their insides and outsides for propaganda purposes. With the blessing of the Ministry of Supply, I wrote and illustrated a paperback about tanks (*Tanks, their place in modern warfare*). This funny little book sold 30,000 copies. So, down the years it has gone; so it goes still.

A few years ago, under commission, I went to Kathmandu to design and paint a mural in the Sheraton Hotel there. The 6 by 18 foot work was a different challenge and deeply satisfying to me.

While there I held an exhibition of my watercolours, and its private view was opened by the British Ambassador, Sir Anthony Hurrell. Earlier, when we were introduced, he opened his eyes, paused, 'BV!' he said. It turned out that he was an ardent

Mixed has been my life as a professional artist; its constant thread has been painting and, when I could strive to get at it, sculpture. Painting I do in oils, watercolour, pastel - and of course drawing, that lovely means of expression, the proper foundation for all the painter's art.

By the fashionable world of 'contemporary art', drawing has been condemned and cast aside. It is no longer considered to be of any importance. I suppose that has been just as well because so few of the practioners of 'contemporary art' seem able to do it. How grateful I am that in my far-gone student days drawing was treated as the most important basic part of an artist's training.

In recent years my painting has developed into a theme in which figures and landscape are interwoven - sometimes with a slightly mystical element - as though something beyond my conscious self takes control. My daughter - appreciatively - refers to them as my 'nutty period'.

And now, for as many more years as I have left, I ask no more than that I may continue to be

angler for coarse fish in his native Norfolk. We got on famously and had much to talk about.

Even now I have not entirely given up what in my youth was called commercial art, now, more deferentially called 'graphics'. Today I find it pleasant and stimulating to design such things as baggage labels for Sheraton Hotels.

busy, continue to enjoy ample work, and to be able to punctuate that with good fishing. At this moment of writing I am in a state of poignant impatience. The new trout season opens in a few weeks.

Bernard Venables

1907 Born in London.

1913 Taken to live in the country at Romney Marsh, Kent. First experience of fishing.

1923 Became an art student.

1926 At end of year ended student life.

1927-29 Sought living as professional artist.

1929 First job in commercial art studio.

1930 Joined Baynard Press as artist-designer.

1931 Left Baynard Press. Became freelance artist.

1931-33 Designing posters for shipping companies, Southern Railway, etc.

1933 Commissioned to design and execute large murals for exhibition stand of Mather and Crowther at the advertising Exhibition at Olympia.

1933 About this time began exhibiting at Royal Academy. Thereafter exhibited intermittantly for a number of years.

1935 Entered hospital for operation. Was there for four months having survived against all expectation.

1935 Began to work for Fleet Street both as artist and writer. As writer contributed to *Christian Science Monitor*, *Time Tide*, etc. As artist contributed to *The Star*, *Evening Standard*, *News Chronicle*, *London Mercury*.

1937 Began fishing the River Wye. Joined *Daily Express* as artist.

1940 First fished Aldermaston lake and River Kennet.

Making cartoon films at Ealing studios. Involvement in London Blitz great fire of London.

1942 First experienced mayfly fishing on Kennet at Hungerford.

1942 Drew aircraft and tanks for progaganda purposes. Produced small book about tanks for Ministry of Supply.

1943 Worked in studios of Ministry of Information; by night at the *Daily Express*. Subsequently worked freelance for Ministry as artist. Designed exhibition stands for Ministry of Information.

1944-45 Working as artist and writer on *Daily Express*.

1945-46 War over. Produced crime cartoon for *Daily Express*.

1946 Joined *Daily Mirror*.

1947 In January started Mr Crabtree as angler. Appointed *Daily Mirror* Angling Correspondent. Ran *Daily Mirror* angling competitions. First broadcast on radio and television.

1953 Left *Daily Mirror* to co-found *Angling Times*. First publication of *Angling Times* on 10 July.

1959 Fishing off Madeira caught biggest shark ever taken on rod and line in Northern Hemisphere.

1962 Left *Angling Times*.

1963 July. First publication of *Creel* magazine.

1963-4 Made *Angler's Corner* series of films (shown

twice on BBC2, then twice on BBC1).

1964 Left *Creel* magazine in December.

1965 To Zambia to make three BBC films about angling. Many subsequent visits to Zambia.

1965-66 Two seasons with the open-boat whalers of the Azores.

1968 First of two walking expeditions to source of Zambezi River.

1969 Appointed Angling Consultant to BOAC.

1970 To Mauritius, Bermuda, Bahamas, to report to BOAC on potential for angling tourism.

1971 To Seychelles, then to Lake Turkana in Kenya to report on potential for angling tourism.

1977 To Tanzania to report to Sheraton Hotels on potential for marine game fishing. Arrested and retained for being a spy!

1982 To Djibouti to explore marine game fishing potential for Sheraton Hotels.

1985 To Kathmandu to paint a mural in the Everest Sheraton Hotel.

There have been various other foreign trips to explore fishing over the past thirty years or so, including Morocco, Gibralter, Romania, Norway, Seychelles, Sweden, Uganda. At various times freelance writer for The Times, Sunday Telegraph, Esquire magazine, Sunday Express magazine, Financial Times.

Also written by Bernard Venables

Tanks: their place in modern warfare, 1942, Country Life.

Fish and Fishing, 1948, Puffin Books.

A Fisherman's Testament, 1949.

Mr Crabtree Goes Fishing, 1949, Daily Mirror.

Fishing (British sports: past and present series), 1953, Batsford.

Guide to Angling Waters, 1954, Daily Mirror.

The Gentle Art of Angling, 1955, Max Reinhardt.

The Angling Times Book, edited with Howard Marshall, 1955, James Barrie.

The Anglers Companion, 1958, George Allen and Unwin.

Mr Cherry and Jim series:

Fishing For Roach, 1961, Angling Times.

Fishing For Pike, 1961, Angling Times.

Fishing For Trout, 1962, Angling Times.

Fishing For Perch, 1962, Angling Times.

Freshwater Fishing, 1967, Herbert Jenkins.

Coming Down the Zambezi, 1974, Constable.

The Piccolo Fishing Book, 1981, Piccolo Books.

Baleia! the Whalers of the Azores, 1968, Bodley Head and Knopf.

Mr Crabtree Goes Fishing, facsimile reprint, 1990, Unwin Hyman.

The following books are also published by

———————

Merlin Unwin Books
21 Corve Street, Ludlow
Shropshire SY8 1DA

The Secret Carp

Chris Yates

It is every carp angler's dream to discover a long-neglected, overgrown lake which holds monster carp, and to be the first person to fish the water in living memory.

Chris Yates found himself in just such a fortunate position and he tells the fascinating story of how the mysteries of the lake and its giant residents slowly revealed themselves to his investigations with rod and line.

This, the author's first book to focus exclusively on carp fishing, contains many insights into the secretive behaviour of this king of freshwater fish, insights which come from someone who has spent a large part of his life in damp sleeping bags beside carp lakes waiting, watching and stalking his chosen quarry.

Full of moments of great angling drama, *The Secret Carp* is also a wonderful account of a magical summer on an English lake.

'Unquestionably the read of the year, indeed of many years. It is a potential classic'.　　　The Times

'The Secret Carp is not just a great angling book, it is perhaps one of the three best fishing books ever written'.　　　The Field

'One of the few books that can suggest to an outsider what the point of fishing might be'.　The Independent

Price: £16.95　ISBN 1 873674 05 8

A History of Flyfishing

Conrad Voss Bark

With a delightful blend of wit and erudition, Conrad Voss Bark tells the story of flyfishing, from the Macedonian 'plumes' of old to the hairwing streamers of today.

He spotlights the sport's formative protagonist's - Juliana Berners, Robert Venables, Isaak Walton, Charles Cotton, Alfred Ronalds, George Kelson, J.C.Mottram, Dr Bell and many others, using his journalists' skills to apppraise the prevailing dogmas, the breakthroughs in tackle and to re-live the great debates and controversies, including the famous Skues-Halford dispute.

Not since Waller Hills' classic *History of Fishing for Trout* has this fascinating sport been tackled with such individual style and verve.

'To a writer with less wit and erudition, covering some 2000 years of subject matter in 200 pages would be a tall order, but Voss Bark manages it with typical aplomb. Evocative, quirky and enjoyable'.
Daily Telegraph

'An enchanting and learned book...We must be thankful for this delightfully illustrated, well-written mine of information from Conrad Voss Bark'.　　The Field

Price £25　ISBN 1 873674 03 1

Trout & Salmon Rivers of Ireland *second edition*

Peter O'Reilly

This deeply-researched guide to the rivers of Ireland is a must for all game anglers. Peter O'Reilly has painstakingly checked and updated all the information contained in the successful first editon.

The rivers are described in great detail - their geographical characteristics, the most productive stretches, game species present, stock levels and average size, catch records when known, local permit requirements (names and addresses given whenever possible), best flies to use, open and close season dates, best fishing times in the year - and much more.

Ordnance Survey references accompany each river entry and detailed location maps (many showing bridges, beats, access roads, etc.) are provided for every significant river in the Republic and Northern Ireland, enabling the angler to plan fishing expeditions in meticulous detail.

Peter O'Reilly is Angling Officer at the Central Fisheries Board and is widely recognised as a leading authority on Ireland's trout, seatrout and salmon fishing.

'This book meets all the criteria by which an angling guide must be judged. It provides exactly the information the prospective angler needs: ther how, the where, the when...information he can waste hours or days trying to find out'.   Trout & Salmon

Price £16.95   ISBN:1 873674 01 5

The Pursuit of Wild Trout

Mike Weaver

This beautifully illustrated book from one of Britain's leading writers on wild trout fishing is for the angler who places quality before mere size, who regards beautiful scenery as a vital ingredient in the fishing day and who is happy to practice 'catch-and-release' in the interest of maintaining stocks of wild fish.

Mike Weaver is a thoughtful and experimental angler and his tactics for out-witting 'wildies' - whether brown, rainbow, brook or cutthroat - are always practical and clearly presented.

From the Tamar, Lyn and Teign in the West Country, to the rainbow-breeding Derbyshire Wye, to the limestone Suir in Ireland and some exciting trout rivers in the USA - the geographical range of this book is wide - Mike Weaver always draws on his first-hand experience.

He discusses the use of barbless hooks, deep wading, innovative fly-tying techniques to 'match the hatch', the classic standard patterns and a variety of stream fishing methods that really do catch trout.

'A splendid book for those wishing to fish for wild brown trout on rivers. I have rarely seen such fine pictures of rivers, tackle, fish and flies'.   The Flyfisher

Price £16.95   ISBN:1873674007

The One That Got Away

or tales of days when fish triumphed over anglers

With original woodcuts by Christopher Wormell

The one that got away is the best-known phrase in fishing. Every angler has at least one story of being outwitted by a huge fish.

This is a collection of original stories from well-known angling enthusiasts and writers. They tell of unforgettable fish hooked and lost, of glimpsed monsters which haunt the imagination and draw the narrator back to a particular lake or river, time and again, in search of a re-match.

David Steel loses his first-ever salmon after an epic struggle on the Ettrick, George Melly is upstaged by a giant Usk brown trout, Jeremy Paxman describes a hilarious adventure in Sri Lanka, Max Hastings battles it out on the Naver, Bernard Venables - extending the definition of 'fish' - describes a thrilling but tragic whaling adventure in the Azores. Chris Yates, holder of the British carp record, tells of his close encounter with an even bigger carp, David Profumo is humiliated by a 400lb shark, Brian Clarke has his angling life marked by a monster pike and Conrad Voss Bark actually helped his fish get away - and he swears it came back to say 'thank you'.

The pens of sixteen of the finest fishing writers have been at work and the result makes compelling reading for anglers of every persuasion.

I couldn't put this book down. It is a marvellous collection of stories - if fish didn't escape then angling wouldn't be what it is. Scotland on Sunday

Price: £16.95 ISBN: 1-873674-02-3

An Angler for all Seasons

the best of H. T. Sheringham

H.T. Sheringham ranks among the finest fishing writers of the twentieth century. Here is a collection of the very best of his angling experiences, taken mainly from his six fishing books and from *The Field*, for which he was angling editor.

No fish escaped his interest, even if it did sometimes escape his creel - carp, tench, chub, pike, roach, salmon and trout - all were pursued with equal gusto.

He takes the reader on a journey without frontiers, from the reservoirs (Blagdon in its opening years) to the finest chalkstreams in England, from overgrown canals to Welsh salmon rivers. No snob, he knew only the joy of the sport.

He is funny, he is moving and - most rare - he is modest about his all-round skills with rod and line. If you are new to Sheringham, *An Angler for all Seasons* will convert you into one of his many admirers.

The essays in this anthology have been chosen and introduced by Tom Fort, the angling correspondent of the *Financial Times*.

'Sheringham was an all-rounder, devoid of snobbery, and a stylist with a sense of humour. He had a novelist's eye for detail and the naturalist's feel for immanence. There is now no excuse for any angler to be ignorant of his output'. Daily Telegraph

Price £16.95 ISBN: 1 873674 04 X

The River Within

A life of Fly-Fishing

William B. Currie

This book distils the fruits of Bill Currie's rich experience of fishing for trout, seatrout and salmon in his much-loved home waters of Scotland, and further afield in Europe and America. Many of the landscapes and waters he fishes are wildernesses, solitary places of rare appeal. He writes of his many journeys and adventures in search of game fish, of his own fascinating fishing life, his philosophy for the sport, and his views on the ever-perplexing behaviour of the fish themselves.

This is a mature collection of writings based on a long and varied fishing life.

It will particularly appeal to those who fish for salmon and seatrout on the rivers and lochs of Scotland. On this subject there can be few writers with such a depth and range of experience as Bill Currie. So, to accompany him on a series of fishing expeditions is not only to gain an insight into the author's fishing and the fish he is after, but also to identify some of the inner satisfactions that the sport of angling can bring, the pleasures of 'the river within'.

Price £16.95 ISBN 1 873674 10 4

The Anglers' Co-operative Association

Bernard Venables has always been in the forefront of those concerned for the environment. He has always supported the Anglers' Co-operative Association.

The ACA was founded in 1958 to fight water pollution on behalf of anglers and other conservationists. It has done so with great success ever since. In the early days, the battles were invariably against industrialists who saw our waterways as convenient conduits into which to tip their waste products. This is no longer the case. The face of pollution is changing, as are agricultural practices, so that now, streams far away from industrial complexes are at risk from the wastes from intensive farming of pigs, cattle and even, by a cruel irony, from fish farms.

Rivers are being polluted by discharges from abandoned coal mines. They are being reduced to shadows of their former glory by our ever-more voracious appetite for water.

Lakes are being altered, for the worse, by insufficiently treated sewage discharges. These enrich the waters and algal blooms occur.

Each of these problems is being tackled by the ACA from its tiny headquarters at 23 Castlegate, Grantham, Lincolnshire, NG31 6SW. Will you please help in the fight by joining as a member?

As Bernard Venables has stated in his foreword: 'If we can save our waters from all that threatens them, I think the older, simpler joy of angling can regain its hold'.

Allen Edwards, Director of the ACA